Touring Cumbria and the Lake District

by

Ralph Wilkinson

Dalesman Books
1985

The Dalesman Publishing Company Ltd.,
Clapham, via Lancaster, LA2 8EB.

First published 1985

ISBN: 0 85206 830 1

Cover photograph of Coniston
by S.C. Sedgwick.
Maps and uncredited photographs
by the author.

Printed in Great Britain by Fretwell & Brian Ltd.,
Goulbourne Street, Keighley, West Yorkshire BD21 1PZ.

Contents

1. Introduction

THERE is no doubt that the best way — some would say the only way — to get to know an area is on foot. It is with some misgivings, therefore, that I make a modest contribution to the considerable volume of literature written specifically for the motorist. I am conscious, however, that there are many who, despite the high costs of motoring, simply enjoy touring by car, whilst there are some who, through age, infirmity or physical disability, would be unable by any other means to enjoy the wonderful variety of scenery which the British countryside has to offer.

It appears to me from observation that the majority of tourists, other than those travelling on organised coach tours, prefer to stay for a few days in a single centre rather than to move on each day and find fresh accommodation each night. In view of this, I have divided the region into three areas each based on a convenient centre from which a number of separate day trips can be undertaken, preferably interspersed with "rest" days. Link routes have been provided for those wishing to consider a two (or even three) centre holiday.

To do justice to the day trips, as long a day as possible should be allowed for each one. The routes described are full of places of interest and things to see — historic houses, castles, churches, museums, towns, villages, beauty spots and viewpoints — so that plenty of time is needed to enable one to get out of the car and explore.

Many of the roads covered are unsuitable for towing caravans. It is assumed that readers will leave their caravans on sites when undertaking day tours by car. Where roads are unsuitable for caravans on link routes, possible alternatives are given. For those who wish to hire a car in the area, the nearest railway station is given.

The book is not meant to be a comprehensive guide; the routes chosen are intended to be representative of the best that the region has to offer. Industrial areas and conurbations are generally avoided, though I am aware that these areas contain much of our rich heritage, especially by way of museums, art galleries, churches and secular buildings. However, many readers probably live in such areas and wish to use the car to "get away from

Holiday Lakeland. The "Raven" approaches the pier at Glenridding, Ullswater. *(F. Leonard Jackson)*

it all". Others will claim, no doubt justifiably, that some of the places omitted are just as full of interest to the tourist as some of those included.

It is hoped that the book will be used by those living in the region as well as by those from outside it. It is a fallacy to believe that if one lives in a region one "knows" it; the book will almost certainly reveal surprises to locals as well as to visitors.

Road numbers, information concerning road signs and other driving instructions are those which were applicable on my latest visit, but such items are subject to change and the information can quickly become out of date. Similarly, opening times and days are liable to alteration and should be checked. The information given is usually that which is applicable in the main tourist season, i.e. late spring/summer.

Although the tours described in the book cover both the popular and lesser-known places, it should be possible to avoid traffic congestion by choosing one's times carefully. I hope that those visiting the region for the first time will be encouraged to return and explore it at greater leisure — perhaps on foot.

2. Cumbria

I WILL resist the temptation to describe Cumbria as England's most beautiful county, but if another were to do so (as, no doubt, many have done) I could not deny it. What is indisputable is that it contains England's highest mountains and largest lakes; however, it is not the size of its features but the almost indescribably beautiful combination of lakes, mountains, valleys, woodlands, rocks and streams which makes Cumbria so distinctive and memorable.

There is a tendency to think of Cumbria and the Lake District as being synonymous, but this is far from the case. Indeed, the Lake District National Park occupies less than one-third of the total area of Cumbria (866 out of 2,658 square miles). A glance at a map of the county shows that a sizeable area of mainly agricultural and forest land lies north of the Irthing to the north-east of Carlisle, whilst further south the River Eden runs for over sixty miles in a quiet valley between the Pennines and the Lakeland Fells. Either the Eden or Irthing valleys would provide the outstanding beauty spots if they were in many other British counties, but in Cumbria they play second fiddle to the Lake District.

How can one attempt to describe the Lake District? It is impossible to do so adequately; no amount of words can convey the magic of the district as effectively as a single personal visit. But there has been no shortage of writers associated with the area: the Wordsworths, Southey, de Quincey, Hartley Coleridge, Harriet Martineau, John Ruskin, Hugh Walpole, Arthur Ransome, Beatrix Potter, Norman Nicholson, Melvyn Bragg . . . the list quickly becomes a catalogue. Sir Walter Scott had close associations with the northern part of Cumbria. The forerunner of many guidebooks to the area was Thomas West's *Guide to the Lakes* published in 1778.

The Lake District is remarkably compact. Within an area of less than 100 miles circumference and 30 miles diameter are over 60 lakes (including 15 "major" ones) and over 180 mountains (i.e. more than 2,000 feet in height) of which four exceed 3,000 feet. Wordsworth observed that the structure of the Lake District was like a cartwheel with spokes radiating from a "hub" in the region of Scafell. Geologists describe it as a dome which is still being

Watendlath bridge. Fast-flowing water rushes down from the high fells before plunging into Derwentwater. *(Frank & Molly Partington)*

eroded. The dome was thrown up several million years ago, but some of the rocks were originally laid down as sediment 500 million years ago. The oldest rocks, the Skiddaw slates, lie to the north and west of the region, whilst the newest (Silurian) rocks lie mainly to the south and east of Windermere. Between them lies a belt of volcanic rocks, known as Borrowdale Volcanics. Thus the landscape consists of three different types: the smooth mountains to the north and west; the craggy mountains of the centre; and the softer landscape to the south and east. The whole has been affected by glaciation in recent times (approximately 10,000 years ago).

One superlative which the tourist authorities naturally play down is the fact that the Lake District contains the wettest place in England. The western rain-bearing winds meeting the hills provide not only the rainfall but also the soft air and rich foliage. Some would claim that the mountains are at their most typical when their peaks are lost in rolling cloud. Often, however, the rest of Cumbria is dry and even sunny whilst rain is falling over the fells. The district as a whole is at its sunniest and driest in springtime and at its wettest in autumn, but there are exceptions and inconsistencies. Indeed, in more than one recent season which over the country as a whole has been regarded as a "wet" summer the Lake District has suffered from drought and a water shortage.

The climate has contributed to the wide range of colour to be enjoyed in the Lake District. The rich green bracken of summer becomes russet brown in winter, whilst the sight of yellow daffodils on a spring day set against a green-grey background with snow-covered mountains in the distance is never to be forgotten. Equally memorable are sunsets over both the lakes and the Cumbrian coast.

In addition to a variety of scenery, the Lake District offers a choice of sports and physical activities, amongst the more popular being sailing, water-skiing, canoeing, walking, mountaineering, rock-climbing, skiing, fishing, swimming, gliding, beagling, fox-hunting, shooting and fell-racing. A peculiarly local sport is Cumberland wrestling. Botanists, naturalists and ornithologists find much of interest in the flora and fauna of the district. After farming, tourism is the largest "industry" in the area.

It is not surprising, therefore, that in recent years much attention has been turned to the problems created by visitors. There is a school of thought which believes that by their very numbers the visitors are destroying the solitude and special charms which they have come to seek. Whilst this may be true of the more popular spots in the height of the season, it is always possible with a little effort to escape the crowds, even on the busiest of days. Nevertheless, the Lake District Planning Board has the unenviable task of trying to balance the interests of farmers, residents and visitors and to spread the pressure points in terms of both times and places.

An early preservationist was Canon Hardwicke Rawnsley, founder of the Lake District Defence Society and one of the co-founders of the National Trust, of which he was secretary from its formation in 1895 to his death in 1920. Today, the Trust is one of the major land owners in the Lake District,

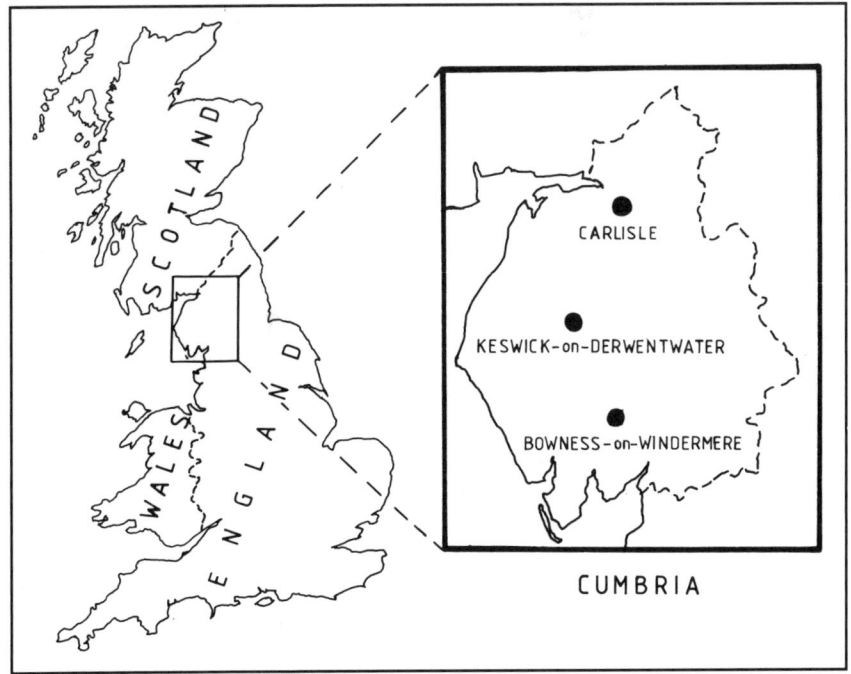

CARLISLE

KESWICK-on-DERWENTWATER

BOWNESS-on-WINDERMERE

CUMBRIA

having in its care over 130,000 acres (built up from innumerable gifts) and 15,000 sheep! A simple plaque at Friar's Crag, Keswick was erected in memory of Canon Rawnsley.

Cumbria today has its own Tourist Board. A glance at the Board's publications reveals a multitude of opportunites available to the visitor; its excellent *Leisure and Holiday Planning Map* lists over 500 locations of places of interest. The independently published and well-produced thrice-yearly *Preview of Lakeland* gives details of opening hours and admission charges to over 170 historic houses, museums, art galleries, etc, in addition to containing a calendar of local events and a "Wining and Dining" guide. Magazines such as *Cumbria* and *Lakescene,* both published monthly, help to keep Cumbrians and visitors informed on happenings in the county. A notable feature of Cumbria is the number of imaginative ventures such as the Theatre in the Forest at Grizedale, the Rosehill Theatre near Whitehaven, the Stanwix Arts Centre at Carlisle and the Brewery Arts Centre at Kendal as well as the large number of amateur dramatic groups.

But Cumbria is still first and foremost an agricultural county. Sheep farming is still predominant, though the traditional Herdwick breeds have now been largely replaced by the more profitable Swaledales. Hill farmers can still be found counting their sheep in the local dialect: "Yan . . . tan . . . tethera . . ." In contrast to the Lake District, the rich soil of the Eden Valley provides the basis for arable farming. The valley is also a centre for dairy and beef farming as are the lowlands between the mountains and the Solway. Fruit growing (especially damsons) takes place in the Lyth Valley.

Cumbria's industries tend to be concentrated around the perimeters of the county. The towns of Maryport, Workington, Whitehaven, Millom and Barrow-in-Furness cling to the coast and owe their industrial development to the proximity of coal and iron ore. Apart from Carlisle, the older market towns (e.g. Appleby, Cockermouth, Kendal, Keswick and Penrith) have not developed substantially, though each has its own local, specialist small industries. Numerous cottage industries and "one-person-craft-centres" are to be found spread across the county.

The earliest traces of man in Cumbria date from the Mesolithic period (8,000 to 3,000 B.C.). These were followed by Neolithic men of the Stone Age whose traces can best be seen in the numerous remains of stone axes from the the axe "factory" in Langdale, whose products have been found scattered over a wide area. Stone circles (sometimes known as "Druids' Circles") exist at Little Salkeld ("Long Meg and her Daughters"), Castlerigg, near Keswick and Swinside, near Broughton-in-Furness, whilst near Eamont Bridge can be found two large circular amphitheatres or "henges" (Mayburgh and "King Arthur's Table"). Iron Age remains are more scanty; the hill-fort on Carrock Fell is a notable exception.

Cumbria contains much evidence of the Roman occupation. The most outstanding monument is, of course, Hadrian's Wall, which enters the county from the east at Gilsland on the Northumberland border and extends to Bowness-on-Solway. The remains of the 5-acre fort at Birdoswald are particularly impressive. A series of defences ran from the wall down the coast to Ravenglass, which has the western extremity of the remarkable Roman road from Ambleside via the spectacularly-sited Hardknott Fort. Another Roman road was "High Street", which can still be traced for many miles over the mountains above Haweswater from Troutbeck to Tirril, whilst the main Roman approaches from the south via the Lune Valley and from the east via the Eden Valley met at Brougham.

After the departure of the Romans, Northern Cumbria became the Kingdom of Rheged, which later became part of the Kingdom of Strathclyde. It is said that the last King of Cumbria, Dunmail, was defeated by the Saxon King Edmund in a battle on what is now Dunmail Raise, between Grasmere and Thirlmere. The Vikings made their way into Cumbria mainly from Ireland and the Isle of Man and their influence remains to this day in place names and local dialects. For several centuries, Cumbria was subjected to raids from the Scots. The north of the county contains many fortified farmhouses, churches and pele towers, whilst the layout of Penrith, with its narrow gateways and streets leading to open spaces where cattle could be herded, was influenced by several attacks from the north, especially in the 14th century. The last conventional battle on English soil is claimed to be the one fought at Clifton in 1745.

Local government reorganisation in 1974 restored the old name of Cumbria. Whatever one might think of the results of the 1974 changes in

Brougham Castle and the River Eamont. Cumbria has a rich legacy of ancient buildings — both great and small.

some other parts of the country, Cumbria is one new county where the boundary changes have brought about a more sensible administrative unit compatible with the natural geographical region. The "Three Shire Stone" at the top of Wrynose Pass serves as a reminder of the former nonsensical division of Cumbria into Cumberland, Westmorland and a detached part of Lancashire. One unexpected result of the 1974 changes is that Cumbria now has two National Parks: the Lake District National Park, which falls wholly within the county, and a corner of the Yorkshire Dales National Park, the boundary of which still follows the former West Riding of Yorkshire county boundary in the Dent and Sedbergh areas.

I would not go so far as to suggest that Cumbria should re-establish its own monarchy, but despite the vast improvements in modern communications (including the M6 motorway, the A66 trunk road and the electrified London-Glasgow railway line) giving increased accessibility, the county still retains many of the characteristics of an independent region. Its mountains might not be as high as those of many mountain countries, but their majesty is unsurpassed as is man's respect for them. Its lakes might only be tiny, but their natural beauty, which changes with the seasons, has the therapeutic effect of restoring to oneself a sense of order, perspective and tranquility.

11

3. South Cumbria

Bowness-on-Windermere is accessible from the M6 Motorway:
From the south, leave at Junction 36, then take the A591.
From the north, leave at Junction 40, then take the A592, except for caravans, which should leave at Junction 39, then take the A6 via Kendal.
The nearest railway station is Windermere.

MY definition of South Cumbria comprises all that part of the county south of a line through Ambleside, with a northern extension over the Kirkstone Pass to include Ullswater, Lowther Park and the Lyvennet Valley. As explained in the Introduction, the routes selected are representative rather than comprehensive; I am conscious that the whole of the Furness peninsula and Walney Island have been omitted.

Geologically, the area is mainly comprised of the newer Silurian rocks and its accompanying landscape, but the older volcanic belt is penetrated, especially in "Western Lakeland Mountains Passes". Incidentally, less than half of Cumbria's mountains passes are passable by car; the only way to experience some of the more dramatic ones is on foot.

I first became familiar with South Cumbria when on a holiday at Grange-over-Sands with my parents in 1945. The excitement which I then experienced on first approaching Bowness-on-Windermere via the lakeside road from Newby Bridge on one of Parkers' pre-war motor-coaches has been renewed on each of my many return visits, whether by bus, coach, minibus, car or on foot at the end of the 73-mile long "Dales Way" footpath from Ilkley.

Bowness-on-Windermere

WINDERMERE — 10½ miles long from Lakeside in the south to Ambleside in the north — is England's largest lake. It is also the nearest lake to the main approaches to the Lake District from the Midlands and the south of England. Just north of the midway point, on the eastern shore of the lake, stands Bowness-on-Windermere, probably the best-known of the lakeland resorts on account of its setting and its accessibility.

As its full name implies, Bowness lies on the lake shore, whilst the twin village of Windermere stands on the hillside a mile away. Bowness is much the older of the two; Windermere did not develop until the arrival of the railway in 1847. Thus, St. Martin's church, Bowness is the parish church for Windermere. The original 12th or 13th century church was destroyed by fire in 1480; the present church was built of Silurian rock in 1483 and "restored" in the early 1870s.

The 19th century restoration of St. Martin's involved enlarging the

12

chancel and reconstructing the famous east window. Much of the glass is 15th century or even earlier and some of it is said to have come from Cartmel Priory or Furness Abbey. The top panes feature the coat-of-arms of various local families, including the Washingtons of Warton (North Lancashire), ancestors of the first President of the U.S.A. The "Stars and Stripes" developed from this coat-of-arms. Another window features a piece of glass known as the "Carriers Arms". The church contains an interesting wooden sculpture of St. Martin on horseback, with a beggar beside him, and a number of old books, including two 16th century chained volumes.

The summit of Orrest Head, though only 783 feet high, gives fine views over Windermere lake and the surrounding mountains. It is approached by a gentle zig-zag path starting from opposite Windermere station. A lower view of the lake and mountains can be enjoyed from Queen Adelaide's Hill, which stands on the lake side of Rayrigg Road, Bowness and is owned by the National Trust. The lake shore includes a portion set aside for swimming. Other local viewpoints include Biskey Howe and Post Knott.

Glebe Park, close to the shore in the centre of Bowness, contains tennis courts, a putting green and a fine pitch and putt course. The Lake District Outdoor Pursuits Centre in Fallbarrow Road includes facilities for archery, canoeing, pony trekking and sailing. But it is to the lake that most sportsmen turn, whether their interests be concerned with the contemplative pastime of angling or the exciting sport of water-skiing. The lake is well-stocked with perch and pike, whilst trout and char (for which fishing licences are required) are also to be found, the latter in the deeper waters.

Boating of all kinds is catered for; many types of boat are available for hire, whilst Bowness is the headquarters of the Windermere Yacht Club. One of the best ways of seeing the lake is from the pleasure boats which ply from around the pier. The large motor vessels, run by Sealink(!), provide a regular service between Lakeside, Bowness and Ambleside. It is possible to combine a cruise on the lake with a trip on the 3¼-mile long steam railway which runs through the Leven Valley from Lakeside to Haverthwaite.

Windermere is dotted with a number of islands. The largest one, the 30-acre Belle Isle, is accessible (except on Fridays and Saturdays) by boat from near Cockshot Point, Bowness. The chief item of interest on Belle Isle is the unusual cylindrical house built in 1774 by John Plaw. It contains portraits by Romney and furniture by Gillow. The remains of a Roman floor were discovered during the building of the house. The admission charge also includes the cost of the boat trip to the island; refreshments are available on Belle Isle.

The Windermere Steamboat Museum in Rayrigg Road, Bowness, houses a fascinating collection of mainly Victorian steam launches, including the *Dolly,* built around 1850 and salvaged from the bed of Ullswater in 1962. Visitors to the museum may take a trip by steam launch from the museum's own private jetty. Bowness Information Centre includes a lecture theatre where illustrated talks and audio-visual presentations are given.

The Lake District National Park Visitor Centre at Brockhole, three miles

Bowness-on-Windermere — among the best-known of the Lakeland resorts on account of its setting and accessibility.

north of Bowness, should not be missed. This converted mansion was built in 1900 by a Manchester businessman. In 1969 it opened as the first National Park Centre in the country. It is open daily from mid-March to mid-November and provides an excellent introduction to the National Park. The permanent exhibition telling the story of the Lake District is supplemented by special exhibitions and a varied programme of short illustrated talks (several daily). The Information Centre is set in spacious grounds which reach down to the lake shore. A visit to Brockhole provides the ideal start to a Lakeland holiday.

South Cumbrian Sampler

This tour should be undertaken on a day other than Saturday, when Holker Hall is closed. Brantwood is open daily for most of the year.

OUR run includes samples of fell, coast and lake scenery, with two country houses for good measure. A narrow, twisting road above the Winster valley is followed by a spectacular view of Windermere lake. We call at the select resort of Grange-over-Sands and the ancient village of Cartmel, with its Priory church, before visiting Holker Hall. A delightful drive along Coniston Water takes in Ruskin's home before returning to Bowness via the northern end of Windermere.

Leave Bowness-on-Windermere by the A5074 Kendal Road. After 1¼ miles fork right into the B5360 (signed "Newby Bridge"). On meeting the A592 bear left, then take the first turning left (signed "Cartmel Fell'). The road climbs up past the Ghyll Head Outdoor Pursuits Centre and shortly afterwards Ghyll Head Tarn appears on the right. Continue to follow the Cartmel Fell signs, climbing to 500 feet at Ludderburn, from where the secluded Winster valley appears below on the left. The narrow road calls for great care on the part of the driver, but observant passengers might catch a glimpse of the Kent estuary and Morecambe Bay ahead. Arthur Ransome, author of *Swallows and Amazons,* lived at Low Ludderburn, which stands to the left of the road.

At the Masons Arms Inn, fork left, then, round the next corner, turn right (signed "Cartmel Fell Church 1"). Almost a mile later, turn left and part way down the hill turn left again to **St. Anthony's church.** The church dates from around 1504-5 and contains some beautiful 15th century glass said to have come from Cartmel Priory. St. Anthony, with his pig, features in the left-hand pane of the altar window. The three-decker pulpit dates from 1698. The adjacent church hall was formerly a school; some of the rocks in the playground show signs of having been used as children's slides.

We should now return to the Masons Arms and fork left (signed "Newby Bridge 3½") to climb Strawberry Bank. After 1½ miles, **Gummer's How** rises to the right of the road. From its summit, magnificent views over Windermere lake can be enjoyed. The Forestry Commission has provided a car park and picnic area on the left of the road, a little way down the hill. Even if we do not leave the car, there is a splendid view of the southern end of the lake, looking across to the steamer terminus at Lake Side. The village of Newby Bridge stands near the point where Windermere lake flows into the River Leven. The Barrow monument on Hoad Hill, Ulverston, can be seen straight ahead. The lake, with its steamers and other craft, reminds one of the Rhine valley near St. Goar.

The steep descent brings us to Fell Foot, where turn left into the A592. **Fell Foot Park,** on the right, comprises 18 acres of grounds owned by the National Trust. It contains car parks, caravan sites, an information centre, a cafe, a picnic area, a point for bathing in Windermere and facilities for fishing and for rowing boat and yacht hire.

Take the first turning left off the A592 into the village of **Staveley-in-Cartmel.** Fork left in this quiet spot and pass St. Mary's church on the right. On reaching the A590, turn left; 1¼ miles beyond High Newton, turn right off this wide highway into the B5271 (signed "Lindale"), then after ¼-mile, fork right — still B5271 (signed "Grange"). The road descends through a pretty, wooded valley to **Grange-over-Sands.**

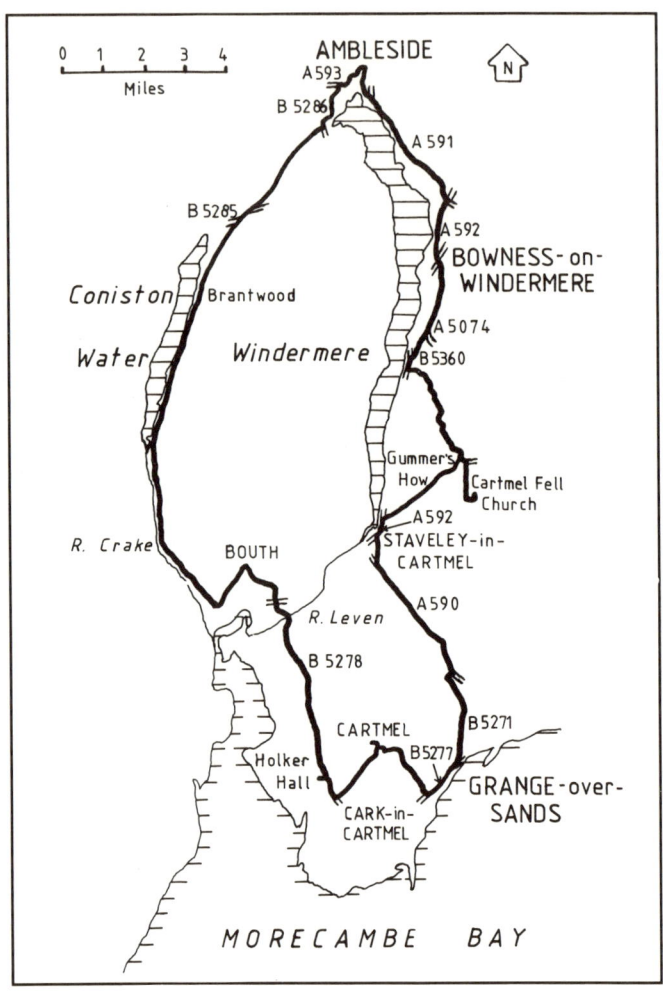

Grange lies in a sheltered spot between the fells and Morecambe Bay. A charming lake, in an ornamental setting, lies between the station and the town centre in an area formerly occupied by the beach. A narrow lane off to the left of the main street by the Hotel Commodore leads to a conveniently situated car park, from which we may explore the resort and from which a narrow path leads across the railway line to the promenade. The railway is hidden from the promenade by rock gardens, the plants of which indicate the mildness of the climate. There is a fine open-air swimming pool situated on the promenade. The town retains the air of a Victorian resort, despite its close proximity to the M6. It boasts of its healthy climate and describes itself variously as "Cumbria's Riviera" and the "Torquay of the North".

Follow the B5277, which bears left into the Esplanade at the Crown Hotel, by the clock tower. The railway has precedence over the road in its proximity to the sea. After one mile, turn right into Cartmel Road (signed "Cartmel 2"), which climbs to High Fell Gate, giving further views over Morecambe Bay, before descending to **Cartmel** village.

A right-then-left turn leads to the Priory Church of St. Mary & St. Michael, which dominates Cartmel. The Priory was founded in 1188 and the monastery remained until the Dissolution in 1537. From its foundation the Priory had also served as the parish church and so, even after the Dissolution, the south aisle continued in use as the parish church, although the remainder of the building was stripped. The church was restored, first by George Preston of Holker Hall in 1618, when the fine oak screen and canopies were placed over the old choir stalls, and again by the 7th Duke of Devonshire in 1859, when the chancel was re-roofed. Most of the early stained glass was destroyed in the years when the building was in ruin, but fragments remain in the Perpendicular east window and in the window of the town (south) choir. The fine south window is modern.

The most extraordinary feature of Cartmel Priory is its tower, which consists of a tower within a tower. The top (inner) tower is set diagonally to the bottom (outer) one and, despite having puzzled architects and engineers, the structure has survived for over 500 years. The church contains a number of rare volumes, including a first edition of Spenser's *Faerie Queene,* printed in 1596.

A little beyond the Priory church, we reach the quaint market square, with its 18th century cross. On the right-hand side is the 14th century gabled gatehouse of the former monastery. This was used as a school from the early 17th century to the late 18th century. It is now owned by the National Trust and houses a craft centre and shop. A large "cruck" barn, adjacent to a cottage dated 1658, houses an exhibition of carved wood sculptures by Michael Gibbon.

Return past the Priory church and keep to the right-hand road (signed "Holker"). At the village of Cark-in-Cartmel fork right to join the B5277, which somewhat inexplicably now becomes B5278. Holker (pronounced "Hooker") Hall lies to the left of the road as we leave Cark.

17

Cartmel village. In the background is the Priory with its curious tower within a tower.

Holker is the home of the Cavendish family, who occupy the old wing. Although the hall dates from the 16th century, the main part open to the public is the new wing, which was built in 1873 to replace the south-west wing, destroyed by fire two years earlier. There are no ropes or barriers to restrict visitors. One is able to explore the building at one's own speed, pausing to examine those items of particular interest without being herded through by a guide. The wing contains much beautiful wood carving, the timber being entirely estate-grown, together with furniture and paintings.

There are attractive views from the hall over the formal gardens and the deer-park, with its large herds of fallow deer. The grounds contain a motor museum, a model railway, a play area and adventure playground, a craft and countryside museum, an animal house, a shop, a cafeteria and picnic areas. The attractions are regularly being added to and special events, such as hot air balloon championships, are held during the summer season. The gardens contains a number of rare shrubs and a fine Chilean monkey puzzle tree, but (as elsewhere in Lakeland) the flowering rhododendrons are the dominant attraction.

On leaving Holker Hall, turn left into the B5278, which runs along the foot of Ellerside and the edge of Haverthwaite Mosses. Cross over the River Leven, then pass through a corner of Haverthwaite village, before crossing the busy A590. Now follow the "Bouth" signs; after ¼-mile (at the

T-junction), turn left. The village of **Bouth** is a proud former winner of the local "best kept village" competition. Keep left at the White Hart Inn and, one mile later, turn right up the hill (signed "Spark Bridge"). After a further mile, we come to the village of **Spark Bridge;** its mill is now the only one left in Cumbria still manufacturing bobbins and reels.

Immediately before the road crosses the bridge, turn right (signed "Nibthwaite"), diligently keeping to the eastern bank of the River Crake. Coniston Old Man and the fells tower majestically ahead as we drive north. At Lowick Bridge, 1½ miles beyond Spark Bridge, repeat the exercise of turning right just before the road crosses the River Crake. Nibthwaite is where Arthur Ransome spent many of his childhood holidays.

One of the prettiest lakeside drives in the country lies ahead. Much of the land east of **Coniston Water** is owned by the National Trust or the Forestry Commission. The latter has provided a car park and relaxation area at Rigg Wood. The trees of Grizedale Forest stretch down to the road on the right, whilst the lake is never far from us on the left. It was on Coniston Water that Donald Campbell made many attempts to break the world water speed record. He was killed on the lake in January 1967, when *Bluebird* crashed at over 300 m.p.h.

Brantwood, the home of John Ruskin from 1871 to his death in 1900, stands to the right of the road near the northern end of the lake. The house was originally an 18th century cottage, which Ruskin bought because of its position and view. He made a number of alterations and extensions including the turret room, built on the corner of his bedroom, and the dining room, with its seven lantern windows representing the seven lamps of architecture. Ruskin, a great admirer of Turner and no mean artist himself, was one of the greatest 19th century writers on art and social reform, but became increasingly insane in his later years and never left Brantwood during the last ten years of his life.

In 1932, the house and 250 acres of the estate were bought by John Howard Whitehouse, who was also responsible for purchasing many of Ruskin's paintings and items of furniture, which he returned to Brantwood where they are now on display. Whitehouse also founded Bembridge School in the Isle of Wight. At the time of writing, there are ambitious plans to return most of Ruskin's drawings, paintings and manuscripts from Bembridge to Brantwood where it is proposed to create a National Ruskin Centre and research library. Work has also started on the estate, which already contains a fine nature trail. An ambitious project to create a 15-acre woodland garden is in hand. There is a tearoom and a good book/gift shop.

One mile beyond Brantwood, keep to the higher (right-hand) road (signed "Hawkshead") and, after a further miles, bear right into the B5285. Take the next turning left and follow the "Ambleside" signs. From the Drunken Duck Inn at Barngates, we have a fine view across the head of Windermere to Ambleside. On meeting the B5286, bear left and, one mile later, cross the River Brathay, then turn right into the A593 at Clappersgate.

Half a mile later, cross Rothay Bridge and turn left, then right (signed

"Windermere"). At Waterhead, pass the northern landing stage for the Windermere steamers and bear right into the A591. Stagshaw Garden (National Trust) stands to the left of the road and, 1½ miles later, we pass the National Park Visitor Centre at Brockhole on the right. On the climb up towards Windermere town from Troutbeck Bridge, turn right into the A592, which leads past Queen Adelaide's Hill back to Bowness.

| DAY TOUR FROM BOWNESS – 2 | # Lowther Park and the Lyvennet Valley |

This is a good tour to fit in with one's other commitments as Lowther Park is open daily.

WE shall climb to the highest point in the Lake District accessible by road, Kirkstone Pass summit (1,489 feet), before descending to follow the northern shore of the District's second largest lake, Ullswater. We visit the fascinating Lowther Wild Life Park, then explore the delightful Lyvennet valley. The return journey passes through the bleak Shap Fells and the valley of the picturesque River Kent.

Take the A592 northwards from Bowness-on-Windermere. After crossing the A591, the road narrows as it climbs up the Troutbeck valley, giving views over Windermere to the left. At Troutbeck church, we cross the Trout Beck; Troutbeck village proper, which contains the 17th century house of Townend (National Trust), lies on the opposite side of the valley. The countryside becomes more barren on the climb up to the **Kirkstone Pass** inn.

I first travelled over the pass in 1953 on a Ribble service bus with a German friend, who was much impressed by the scenery, despite his familiarity with the awe-inspiring grandeur of the Alps. Regular bus services ceased running over the Kirkstone Pass many years ago, but the Mountain Goat company now operates a minibus service, including a "Goat and Boat" trip to Ullswater. I find the surroundings no less foreboding however many times I travel over the pass.

A steep descent (at 25%) with Dove Crag on the left and Raven Crag on the right brings us to Kirkstonefoot. **Brothers Water,** to the left of the road, is almost permanently in shadow. Beyond Brothers Water, the valley widens out a little. Deepdale runs off to the left, then the Goldrill Beck runs alongside us to the right. **Patterdale** is a good point from which to climb Helvellyn; several routes lead to the summit. Another track runs via Grisedale Tarn to Grasmere. St. Patrick is said to have preached and baptised converts in Patterdale. St. Patrick's church, which contains some interesting tapestries, stands to the left of the road. Grisedale runs off to the west just beyond the church.

Ullswater shortly appears on the right, occupying the valley floor between the Helvellyn and High Street ranges. **Glenridding,** formerly a mining community, is a busy, popular spot. Boats sail from here to Howtown (on the southern side of the lake) and Pooley Bridge (at the north-eastern end of Ullswater). It is possible to walk round the lake, splendid views of the head of Ullswater being obtained from Place Fell, opposite Glenridding.

Beyond Glenridding, we pass Stybarrow Crag on the right and Glencoyne Wood on the left. Much of the land in this vicinity is National Trust property. The road now follows the water's edge with superb views of the lake unhindered by walls. Just beyond the junction with the A5091, there is on

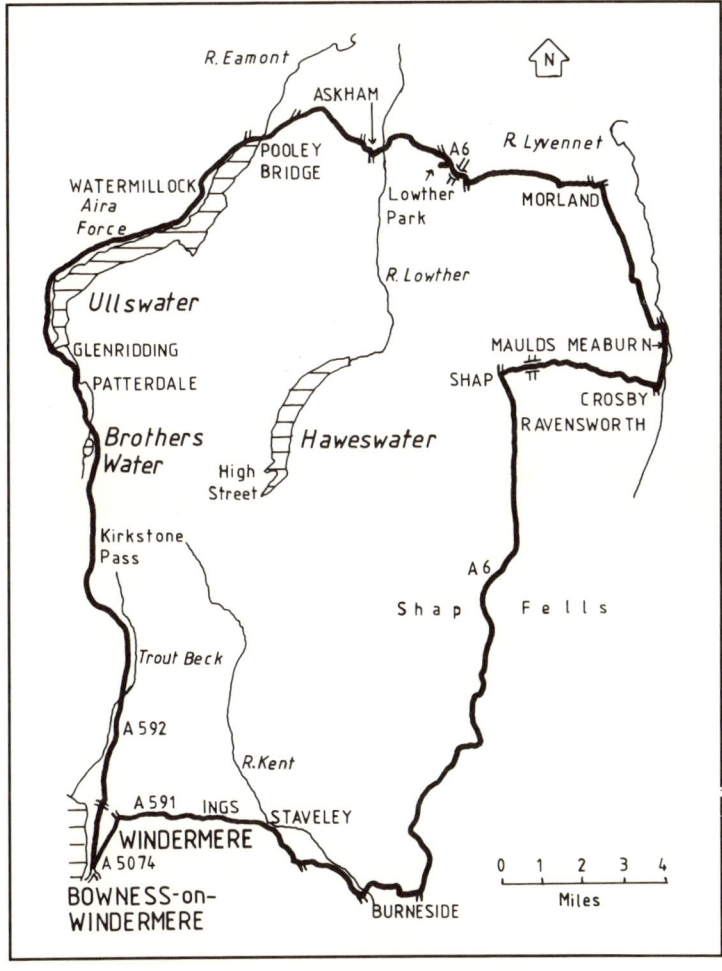

the left of the road a car park from which a footpath leads to **Aira Force** and **High Force**. Both these waterfalls lie in the 700-acre Gowbarrow Park — also National Trust property — from which further fine views of Ullswater can be seen.

Aira Force provided the inspiration for some of Wordsworth's poetry. It was also along this stretch of Ullswater (and not Grasmere) that Wordsworth saw the now immortalised daffodils. The castellated building on the left of the A592 is Lyulph (or Lyulf's) Tower, an 18th century shooting box built by the Duke of Norfolk. The road continues alongside the lake except for a short distance through the village of **Watermillock.** Ullswater is just over seven miles long, its deepest point (over 200 feet) being close to the far shore opposite the Aira Beck. It gradually becomes more shallow towards Pooley Bridge. The lake is the home of the skelly, a kind of herring which lives in the deep fresh water.

At the foot of the lake, fork right into the B5320, which leads past Pooley Bridge landing stage. The village of **Pooley Bridge** stands at the point where Ullswater flows into the River Eamont. It was formerly the home of Thomas Clarkson, the anti-slavery campaigner and a friend of Wordsworth. * Three-quarters of a mile beyond Pooley Bridge, turn right (signed "Celleron ¾")

* A road from Pooley Bridge runs for several miles along the southern shore of Ullswater, but it is not possible to make a complete circuit of the lake by road. I will, no doubt, not be thanked by the powers that be for mentioning this road, as its use appears to be being discouraged, presumably on account of its narrowness. Those who persist in following it — preferably out of high season — are rewarded by a spectacular view over Ullswater from the top of Howtown Hause, a corkscrew rivalling Hardknott and Wrynose for severity as it climbs from Howtown to Martindale church.

and follow a narrow road to Askham. Just beyond the junction with the road from Tirril, we cross the Roman road High Street, appropriately named as it comes directly over the mountains from Ambleside.

On the descent towards Askham village, there are glimpses of the facade of Lowther Castle across the Lowther valley. Cautious driving is well rewarded by the beautiful village of **Askham,** which is spoiled only by the modern development at the entrance. Turn left into the wide main street (signed "Lowther 2"). At the lower end of the street on the left is Askham Hall, which dates from the 14th century and is now the home of the Earls of Lonsdale. On the opposite side of the road just before the bridge is St. Peter's church, a 19th century building built on the site of an earlier church and containing a 17th century font.

After crossing the River Lowther, we enter the 3,000-acre **Lowther estate.** St. Michael's church stands to the left of the road at the top of the first hill. The church contains a curious mixture of architectural styles and periods ranging from the 12th to the 19th centuries. The Victorian Lowther mausoleum stands in the churchyard, from which Askham Hall can be seen across the valley. Until 1936 the Earls of Lonsdale lived at Lowther Castle. The present castle (or what remains of it) was built by Robert Smirks between 1806 and 1811. The roof was removed in 1957, but the 420-foot long north front remains imposing from a distance.

At the top of the hill, keep straight ahead for the **Wild Life Park:** Lowther estate village stands to the right. At the next (acute-angled) crossroads, again keep straight ahead, then on meeting the A6 turn right into the village of Hackthorpe. A sharp right-hand turn (signed "Lowther ½") leads to the entrance gates to the 130-acre Adventure Park. It is possible to drive right through the park, but dogs must be left in specially provided kennels at the entrance. The park contains over 60 species of birds and animals, including waterfowl, cranes, flamingoes, wild boars, foxes, otters and badgers as well as deer, which have inhabited the estate for centuries.

On returning to the A6, turn right, cross over the M6 motorway, then immediately turn left* (signed "Great Strickland ½"). Pass under the London-Glasgow railway on its northbound descent from Shap summit and follow the "Morland" signs through the village of Great Strickland and along quiet country lanes. The Pennine Fells appear ahead, with High Cup Nick sandwiched between Dufton Pike and Murton Pike.

The road now descends to **Morland.** St. Laurence's church, which stands to the left at the entrance to the village, is built on the site of an earlier (10th century) timbered hall. The tower dates from pre-Conquest (11th century) times and is the only one of this period in Cumbria, whilst the church itself

---

* The route can be shortened by taking the A6 south to Shap.

Glenridding from the Dodd. This bird's-eye view gives a good impression of the head of Ullswater and distant Patterdale stretching away towards Kirkstone Pass. *(James E. Tiffin)*

has undergone a number of alterations and restorations. A useful hand-bat guide in the church gives a summary of the major changes and lists other items of interest, including the Jacobean communion rail, the fragments of 17th century box pews, the 1662 font and cover, the 1721 pulpit, the palimpsest memorial to John Blyth (both sides of which can be seen by pressing a button) and the 20th century east window and reredos. On entering Morland, bear right at the first junction (near the church), left at the next junction, then right again by the Crown Inn into a pretty lane with a stream running alongside.

Follow the "Maulds Meaburn" signs along further pleasant country lanes with an attractive wooded section. As we turn right into **Maulds Meaburn** village, Meaburn Hall stands to the right. This delightful building, which dates from 1610, was the ancestral home of the Lowthers before they moved to Lowther Castle. In the garden stand two old stone summer-houses. Maulds Meaburn is a picturesque village with roadside greens and the tiny River Lyvennet running through the middle. At the time of writing, an ancestral research centre and recreation centre is being created at nearby Holesfoot.

St. Lawrence's church, **Crosby Ravensworth,** stands to the right of the road, approached after crossing an ancient, narrow bridge over the stream. This miniature cathedral dates from the 12th century, but has seen many later additions and alterations. The remains of an even older cross stand in the churchyard; the village is said to take its name from a 7th century cross around which early Christians gathered, led by St. Paulinus. In the vicinity of Crosby Ravensworth are the remains of Iron Age and Bronze Age villages and burial mounds.

Take the first turning right beyond the church (signed "Shap 3½") and climb up a winding road out of the Lyvennet valley. Helvellyn and the Lake District mountains re-appear ahead dramatically on the approach to Shap. Cross over the M6 motorway and descend to the village where, on meeting the A6, turn left. **Shap** is a rather bleak community, best-known for its quarries and its ruined 12th century abbey. Little now remains of the abbey other than the 16th century belfry tower overlooking the River Lowther. Much of the village was built from stones from the abbey.

The road south at first follows the London–Glasgow railway which reaches the highest point on its English section (915 feet) at Shap summit. The once notorious incline, with its fours miles at 1 in 75 when approached from the south, provided a formidable challenge to the steam locomotive, but is hardly noticed by today's modern electric trains. Beyond the Shap Granite Company's works, road and rail diverge. The A6 climbs to almost 1,400 feet before descending (first at 7%, then steepening to 10%) to Hucks Bridge over the Borrowdale Beck. A short rise is followed by a further long descent to the Bannisdale Beck, after which the pattern repeats itself.

Three-quarters of a mile beyond the turning to Whinfell, turn right (signed "Burneside 1½"). The 14th century Burneside Hall, with its pele tower and remains of an impressive gateway, stands to the left of the road at the entrance to **Burneside,** a busy industrial community. At the T-junction, turn right (signed "Bowston 1") and pass the Victorian St. Oswald's church on the right. Now follow the Kent valley through the village of Bowston. After crossing over the railway by a bridge, turn right into the A591, then after crossing back over the railway by a level crossing, enter Staveley.

The Dales Way, the long-distance footpath from Ilkley to Bowness-on-Windermere, follows a particularly attractive riverside course between Burneside and Staveley. Until recently, a number of mills — textile, bobbin, paper and snuff — were strung out along this section of the River Kent, but most have now closed.

Beyond Staveley, the A591 is a fast road to Windermere, but it is worth making a slight detour into the village of **Ings** (which stands immediately to the left of the road) to see its delightful Georgian church, which was built at the expense of Robert Bateman, a local boy who made is fortune in Italy. It contains much Italian marble sent by Bateman.

As we surmount a low hill on approaching Windermere town, enjoy the view of Windermere lake which many thousands of visitors experience as their first glimpse of "The Lakes". Just beyond Windermere station, turn left into the A5074 to return to Bowness-on-Windermere.

<table>
<tr><td>DAY TOUR
FROM
BOWNESS – 3</td><td>

Western Lakeland Mountain Passes

</td></tr>
</table>

This tour includes some of the steepest roads in England and should not be undertaken by inexperienced drivers. Despite the fact a regular minibus service operates over the Wrynose and Hardknott Passes, their severity should not be under-estimated. Muncaster Castle is open daily except Mondays (other than Bank Holidays).

WE shall explore the Langdales before taking the route followed by the Romans over the dramatic Wrynose and Hardknott Passes. This is followed by a drive along secluded Eskdale to the West Cumbrian coast at Ravenglass. Nearby is the spectacularly sited Muncaster Castle with its delightful gardens, whilst the return journey takes in the charming valleys of the River Duddon and the River Leven. We shall encounter both a miniature and a full-sized steam railway in unexpected surroundings.

Leave Bowness-on-Windermere by the A592 (northbound) with Windermere lake on our left; Queen Adelaide's Hill provides an easily accessible viewpoint from which to see much of the lake. On meeting the A591, turn left and descend to Troutbeck Bridge. The National Park Visitor Centre at Brockhole stands between the road and the lake.

Drive northwards towards Ambleside, catching glimpses of **Windermere**

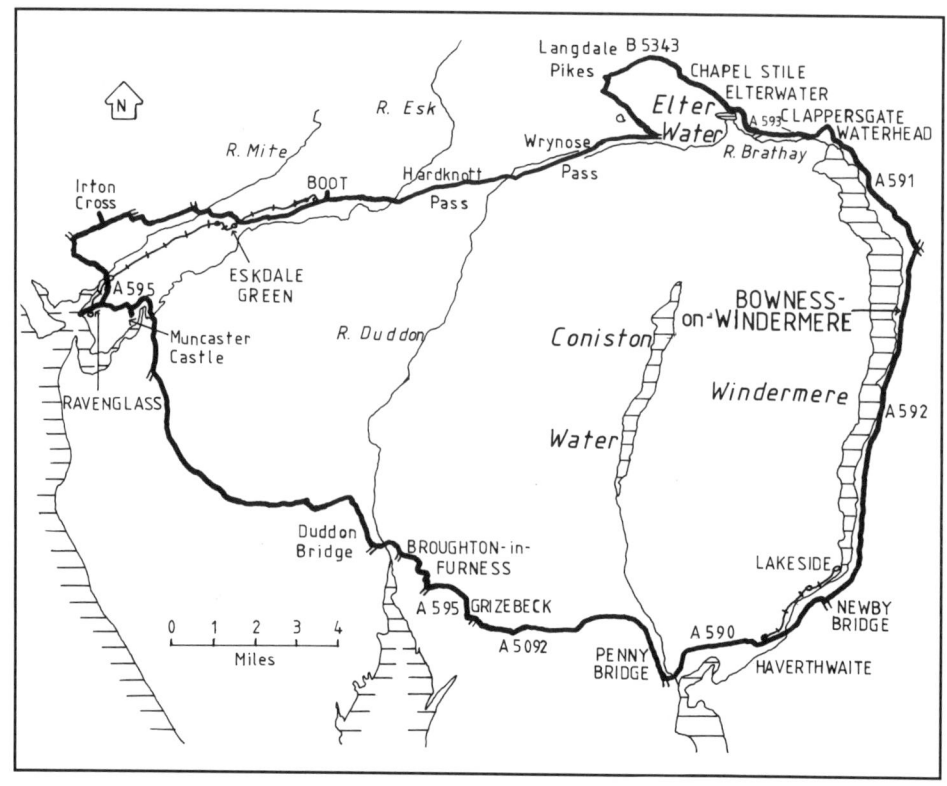

lake through the trees, but it is not until Low Wood that one can comprehend the full splendour and beauty of the northern end of the lake in its setting, with the Langdale Pikes in the background. A mile later, at Waterhead, the northern terminus of the lake steamers, fork left. The road passes the remains of the Roman fort of **Galava** on the left at Borran's Field. This stood on an area of flat land near to where the River Brathay enters the lake. Twenty-one acres of land at Borran's Field are owned by the National Trust. Some of the finds from the fort are housed at Brockhole.

Turn left into the A593, then left again and over the bridge into Clappersgate. At the Skelwith Bridge Hotel, fork right into the B5343. Close by is the **Skelwith Force** waterfall. **Elterwater** lake shortly appears on the left, then there is a view across open country to Elterwater village with the Langdale Pikes in the background. Much of the land around Great Langdale, Little Langdale and Elterwater is owned by the National Trust, Dr. G. M. Trevelyan and Beatrix Potter being among the principal benefactors. Keep straight ahead to Great Langdale through the village of **Chapel Stile,** dominated by the Victorian Holy Trinity Church. There are several quarries in the vicinity. In Neolithic times, Great Langdale housed an axe factory with a prolific output, Langdale axes having been found in many parts of the country.

Great Langdale is a popular valley for walkers and rock-climbers. Crinkle Crags, Bow Fell, Rossett Pike, Pike o'Stickle, Harrison Stickle and Pavey Ark are all within access. The New Dungeon Ghyll Hotel stands at the foot of Mill Gill and close to the spectacular Dungeon Ghyll Force. Beyond Middle Fell, the road turns sharply to the left and at this point the B5343 terminates.

The road now changes dramatically in character as it climbs at 25% (1 in 4) out of Great Langdale. There is a splendid view (for the passengers!) behind us over Great Langdale and the Langdale Pikes. At the summit, **Blea Tarn** appears ahead in its fine mountain setting. Opposite the tarn is a small car park. On the descent, also at 25%, the view ahead is dominated on the right by Wetherlam. At the foot of the hill, turn sharp right (signed "Wrynose") to rejoin the Roman road from Galava (Ambleside) to Glanoventa (Ravenglass).

The road from Great Langdale over into Little Langdale, dramatic though it is, is but a mere "curtain-raiser" compared with what is to follow. Beyond Fell Foot Farm (National Trust owned), we enter the **Wrynose Pass.** On the climb up the pass — again at 25% — passengers have another fine view behind, this time over **Little Langdale,** with Little Langdale Tarn in the floor of the valley. Near the summit of the pass, the Three Shires Stone stands to the right of the road. This formerly marked the meeting point of the counties of Cumberland, Lancashire and Westmorland. From the stone there is a relatively easy walk (to the right of the road) via Red Tarn and Oxendale into Great Langdale or a climb up the Pike of Blisco (2,304 feet), from where magnificent views can be obtained of Crinkle Crags, Bow Fell and the Langdale Pikes.

Another descent at 25% leads to Cockley Beck. Turn right and cross the infant River Duddon with Harter Fell (2,140 feet) dominating the view to the left. The most dramatic scene of all is now about to unfold. The sign indicates a gradient of 30% (1 in 3⅓). We soon leave the Duddon Valley far behind on the steep ascent over the **Hardknott Pass.** The summit of the pass (1,291 feet) is ten feet higher than that of the Wrynose). Beyond the summit, Eskdale opens out below with the Irish Sea in the distance. Eskdale is unusual in that it does not contain a lake.

Three-quarters of a mile past the summit, there is a tiny car park on the right of the road and shortly beyond this a path leads off to the right to **Hard Knott Roman Fort.** This 375-foot square fort, with ramparts 20 feet thick, encloses nearly three acres. It was known to the Romans as Mediobogdum. The first building which we approach is the bath house, beyond which is the fort proper. The fort contains the remains of a number of buildings including the Headquarters' Building, the Commandant's House and various granary buildings. It is well worth proceeding through the north entrance, i.e. the one furthest away from the road, to obtain a breathtaking view across Eskdale to Sca Fell and Sca Fell Pike (3,210 feet), the highest point in

England. From here it is possible to appreciate the extraordinary situation of the fort — almost literally a "castle in the air".

Descend to the foot of the Hard Knott Pass and into the verdant valley of the Esk. Both the road and the landscape are in marked contrast to what has gone before. At Brookhouse, a road leads off to the right to Boot village, but it is a cul-de-sac and there is no car park in the village. **Eskdale Mill,** which stands in Boot village, has been restored to working order by Cumbria County Council and is open to visitors. A permanent exhibition shows the history and techniques of milling and farming activities within the valley. The mill is approached via a 17th century packhorse bridge. (Cars should be parked at Eskdale station, Dalegarth).

A little further along the road stands Eskdale (Dalegarth) station, the present terminus of the **Ravenglass and Eskdale Railway.** This small railway was originally opened in 1876 to carry haematite from the mines above Boot to Ravenglass. The original terminus was in Boot village and the railway was built to a gauge of three feet. It has had a chequered history, having been "rescued" more than once. After being closed for two years, the railway was bought in 1915 by W. J. Bassett-Lowke and converted to a 15-inch gauge. In 1960 it was purchased by a preservation society and its prosperity has grown steadily since. An intensive service of passenger trains is now run by radio control between Ravenglass and Eskdale to cope with the peak season demand.

Eskdale station at Dalegarth is a convenient point from which to visit **Stanley Ghyll** waterfall and nature trail. Beyond Beckfoot the road follows 'La'al Ratty", as the railway is affectionately known, for a short distance. At the King George IV Hotel, two miles beyond Boot, turn right* and enter Eskdale Green. After ¼-mile cross the railway by The Green (formerly Eskdale Green) station. (On one visit to Eskdale it was my intention to travel from Dalegarth to The Green, then walk with one of my sons through the lovely, roadless Miterdale to Miterdale Head. As it was out of season and my son was the only child passenger, he was given a cherished ride on the footplate of the miniature locomotive *River Irt*. Needless to say, we had to travel from Dalegarth to The Green via Ravenglass (!) and shorten the walk).

The village of **Eskdale Green** stands on a low ridge which divides Eskdale from Miterdale. The road winds through the village, passing the Outward Bound School on the right and the lane to Irton Road station on the left. At the Bower House Inn, bear left (signed "Holmrook 3½"). By Irton Hall, a Victorian building incorporating the remains of a much earlier building, turn left (signed "Holmrook 2"). The hall is now a residential school for spastic children. Three-quarters of a mile later a road leads off to the right to Irton Church, best known for the 9th century cross which stands in the graveyard. The 10-foot high cross stands at the back of the church and should not be

*The route can be shortened by turning left at the King George IV and taking the moorland road over Birker Fell, dropping steeply into the Duddon valley at Ulpha. The A595 is joined at Duddon Bridge.

The reed-strewn shores of placid Elterwater. In the distance is the unmistak-able profile of the Langdale Pikes. *(F. Leonard Jackson)*

confused with the modern imitation in the corner of the churchyard.

We must now return to the road and proceed towards Holmrook. On meeting the A595, turn left (signed "Barrow"). Near the turning to Saltcoats, pass Carleton Hall on the left and at **Muncaster Mill** cross the River Mite and "La'al Ratty". The old water mill has been restored to working order by the railway on behalf of the Eskdale Trust. At the top of the ensuing hill, turn right into Ravenglass village.

Ravenglass stands in the joint estuary of three rivers — the Irt, the Mite and the Esk. It was an important port in Roman times. Parts of the bath building, now known as Walls Castle, still stand to a height of over 12 feet, being some of the tallest Roman remains to be seen in Britain. A Roman Heritage Trail has been laid out. In the station yard, the Ravenglass and Eskdale Railway has a museum, which contains a fine model of the former Boot station and incline railway. Part of the British Rail station building is now the Ratty Arms, the bar comprising the former booking hall, ticket office and ladies' room. Between Ravenglass and Drigg is a nature reserve containing a large colony of black-headed gulls.

Ravenglass's single main street is a cul-de-sac, so we must return to the A595 where turn right. The entrance to **Muncaster Castle** shortly appears on the right (car park opposite). The castle stands on the Roman route from Ravenglass to Hard Knott and is strategically sited overlooking the Esk valley. The present building dates form medieval times, but is largely the work of Anthony Salvin (early 19th century). It contains tapestries, silver, china, pictures, books and a fine collection of 16th and 17th century furniture. The King's Bedroom contains a painting of Henry VI with the "Luck of Muncaster", an enamelled 15th century bowl. This was given to Sir John Pennington by the king in gratitude for being given shelter at Muncaster after the Battle of Hexham. The king is said to have been found wandering in the fells by a local shepherd. The spot where they met is marked by an 18th century monument at Chapels, which can be seen from the bedroom window.

The views from Muncaster Castle and its grounds, especially the terrace, are superb. The grounds contain a magnificent and varied collection of rhododendrons and azaleas, several having been brought from the Himalayas. They also include a garden centre, tree trail, nature walks, children's playground and commando course, together with a large collection of animals .and birds, including wallabies, Himalayan bears, pheasants, toucans and flamingoes.

On leaving the castle, continue to follow the A595 which descends to cross the Esk. The slopes of Birkby Fell, which stands to the left of the road, contain the Barnscar settlement — the remains of an early Bronze Age village. The "pepper pot" on top of the hill is said to have assisted smugglers heading for Ravenglass. Some 1¼ miles after crossing the River Esk, keep left (signed "Corney 2, Broughton-in-Furness 10"). On the climb of Corney Fell, there are views of the Esk estuary over to the right, whilst beyond, the Isle of Man can be seen on the horizon, weather permitting.

Ignore the turning to Corney and climb on to open moorland. The view to the right is dominated by the mass of Black Combe. On the approach to the summit, there is a fine view behind looking northwards along the Cumbrian coast towards St. Bees Head. Ahead from the summit there are equally fine views over the Furness Fells. On the descent, a footpath leads off to the right to Swinside Stone Circle. The Duddon estuary can be seen to the right.

A little further along, the **Duddon valley** unfolds to the left, with the central massif of the Lakeland mountains providing the backdrop to the scene. On the lower part of the descent to the River Duddon, the scene changes to one of sylvan beauty. The Duddon valley inspired some 34 of Wordsworth's sonnets. My own appreciation of this part of Lakeland has been enriched by the experience of bringing parties of American students to High Duddon and sharing their enthusiasm for the surrounding countryside.

On rejoining the A595, keep left and cross the River Duddon by Duddon Bridge. The road crosses a series of valleys, marked by level stretches across marshy esturial plains, divided by spurs of much older rocks, marked by steep, twisting inclines. At the top of the next hill, by the High Cross Inn, turn slightly left to enter the town of **Broughton-in-Furness.** This small market town has an interesting square, containing stocks, stone tables for the sale of salmon and other fish and produce, and an obelisk erected by the widow of John Gilpin in 1810 to commemorate the 50th year of the reign of George III. The town charter is publicly proclaimed in the square annually on 1 August. The G.P.O. operates a postbus service from Broughton up the Duddon valley.

Beyond the next ridge, we cross the valley of the Kirkby Pool — "Pool" is the local name for a small river — with views of Coniston Old Man to the left. We climb over a further ridge, with views over the Duddon Channel to the right, then descend into the ancient settlement of Grizebeck. From here take the A5092, which cimbs steeply up the side of a more substantial ridge. The hill to the left, Burney, rises to only 979 feet; it seems much higher because of the long climb up from Grizebeck, but the latter village is almost at sea level. There are views beyond Burney of the Lakeland Fells.

The road descends through the villages of Gawthwaite and Lowick Green into the valley of the River Crake. Beyond Penny Bridge, turn left into the A590. We are now on the edge of Greenodd, a former port exporting slate, lead and copper ore. Keep along the side of the estuary of the River Leven, then cross the valley of Rusland Pool to Haverthwaite.

Haverthwaite station, which stands to the left of the road, is the headquarters of another preserved railway, but a very different one from "La'al Ratty". The **Lakeside and Haverthwaite Railway** is a standard-gauge railway consisting of the truncated tail of the former Furness Railway branch from Plumpton Junction, near Ulverston, to Lakeside. It runs a regular steam-hauled passenger service over the 3½-mile line between Haverthwaite, Newby Bridge and Lakeside, where it connects with the Sealink steamers on Windermere.

Follow the fast, new road through the Leven valley, by-passing the centres of the villages of **Haverthwaite** and **Backbarrow.** The latter was an early industrial settlement. Its ironworks closed in the 1960s after more than 250 years of operation. John Wilkinson, the iron master, was the son of an employee of Backbarrow works. A cobalt blue powder factory now occupies a former cotton mill. A multi-million pound leisure complex is being developed at the time of writing. There are attractive views of the River Leven to our left between Backbarrow and Newby Bridge.

Beyond the Newby Bridge Hotel, turn left into the A592. At Fell Foot, **Windermere** appears in sight on the left. The lake is never very far away and we have occasional glimpses across to the western bank. There is a particularly fine view across to the Lakeside steamer terminus. Return to Bowness by this popular lakeside drive.

DAY TOUR FROM BOWNESS – 4	# West of Windermere

It is advisable to set off from Bowness fairly early in the day to avoid long queues at the ferry and at Hill Top, Near Sawrey. Hill Top opens at 10 a.m. but is closed on Friday. At Hawkshead, the school is closed on Wednesday. Rusland Hall is closed on Saturday and the Coniston "Gondola" does not sail on Saturday morning. Stott Park Bobbin Mill is closed on Sunday morning.

BEATRIX Potter, William Wordsworth and John Ruskin were three dissimilar writers, but all spent much of their lives in the area to the west of Windermere, though not, of course, at the same time. Our route is associated with all three, who were no doubt all inspired by their lake, mountain and woodland surroundings.

Take the A592 Barrow road south from Bowness-on-Windermere and, after ½-mile, turn right into the B5285 (signed "Hawkshead"). After a further ¼-mile, we reach the Windermere Ferry. **Windermere** is less than ½-mile wide at this point, but the leisurely crossing allows one time to take in the lake scenery, including views of Belle Isle to the north (right).

The west bank of Windermere northwards from the ferry to Wray Castle is owned by the National Trust. The Claife estate includes a nature trail and there is public access to the shore of the lake. The road (still B5285) from the ferry runs for a short way along the edge of the lake before climbing up to the village of Far Sawrey. A short distance separates the villages of Far and Near Sawrey; "Far" and "Near" are in relation to Hawkshead.

As we enter **Near Sawrey,** Beatrix Potter's former home and workplace, **Hill Top,** stands to the left of the road. The main part of the house dates from the early 17th century. It contains many of Beatrix Potter's items of furniture, china, pictures and original drawings. To visit the house is to step straight into the pages of her many books. One would hardly be surprised to be greeted by any of the well-known characters — Jemima Puddleduck, Pigling Bland, Tom Kitten, Samuel Whiskers and so on — in the familiar surroundings, many of which are recognisable from the illustrations contained in these children's favourites. Hill Top was bought from the royalties of the *Tale of Peter Rabbit;* the later stories were written here. For most of her rather sad life, Beatrix Potter was a friend of Canon Rawnsley, one of the founders of the National Trust. She left the staggering total of over 4,000 acres of land and much property to the Trust, including Hill Top, half the village of Far Sawrey and various estates in the Coniston, Tilberthwaite, Hawkshead and Troutbeck areas. The Tower Bank Arms, next to Hill Top, is also owned by the National Trust.

Shortly after leaving Hill Top, turn left* (signed "Lakeside 5½") and enjoy the view of **Esthwaite Water** to the right. At the next junction, fork left (again signed "Lakeside") and enter a single track road. In less than a mile, cross the Cunsey Beck and turn left into a wider road. **Graythwaite Hall** stands to the right of the road. The Elizabethan hall, home of the Sandys family, is noted for its seven acres of gardens, which are open in springtime to enable visitors to see the profusion of rhododendrons and azaleas.

Beyond Graythwaite, there are glimpses of Windermere through the trees to the left. We pass the two entrances to the Y.M.C.A.'s Lakeside National Centre, also on the left. Three-quarters of a mile beyond the second entrance is **Stott Park Bobbin Mill,** now an industrial museum in the care of the Department of the Environment. It was a working bobbin-mill from 1835 to 1971 and was one of over sixty in Cumbria in 1850. The machinery on view was used mainly for the manufacture of domestic bobbins.

Turn right immediately past the entrance to the bobbin mill (signed "Rusland 4") and at the next junction bear left into **Finsthwaite.** The village was formerly a centre of besom-making. Its church (St. Peter's) has a squat spire surmounting a sturdy tower and is somewhat Scandinavian in appearance. Beyond Finsthwaite, keep right at each successive junction, following the signs to Rusland Hall. Shortly after emerging from the trees in the beautiful Rusland valley, the hall comes into view ahead. At Rusland, turn left; the entrance to the hall is immediately on the left.

Rusland Hall dates from 1720. It contains a fascinating collection of musical instruments, including self-playing pianos, a self-acting organ and numerous pianolas. Another room contains early photographic equipment, including several cameras and a 1915 cine projector. One upstairs room represents a Victorian nursery, whilst the whole house contains a varied collection of antiques. The landscaped grounds are graced by peacocks, incuding some unusual white ones.

From Rusland, follow the "Satterthwaite" signs, turning left at the T-

*The route can be shortened by following the B5285 alongside the tranquil Esthwaite Water to Hawkshead. This road passes close to the North Fen Nature reserve on the north-east edge of Esthwaite.

junction below the isolated St. Paul's church, then left again, and right by the Quaker meeting house at Rookhow. After crossing Forge Mill bridge, turn left alongside Grizedale Beck, with its pretty waterfalls, and enter **Grizedale Forest.** The forest, which covers over 7,000 acres, is maintained by the Forestry Commission, which is clearly conscious of the interest shown by visitors. Picnic areas, footpaths, forest walks, nature trails, observation towers and hides and a camp site have been provided. The Silurian Way is a 9½-mile long waymarked path. The forest is the home of deer, badgers, foxes and a variety of bird-life.

The road winds through the village of Satterthwaite and just over a mile later comes to Grizedale. A large car park stands on the site of the former Grizedale Hall to the right of the road. The stable block now houses the unusual Theatre in the Forest. During the daytime, the Forestry Commission shows forestry and wildlife films, whilst in the evening the theatre becomes a centre for classical and folk concerts, films, drama and art exhibitions. Another building contains an excellent wildlife museum and visitor centre, whilst deer (note the spelling!) souvenirs are on sale in the shop.

Follow the road through the forest and across Hawkshead Moor. On leaving the forest, there is a splendid view of Windermere (lake) and Ambleside ahead to the left, whilst Esthwaite Water appears nearer at hand below us on the right as we begin to descend the hill which winds down to

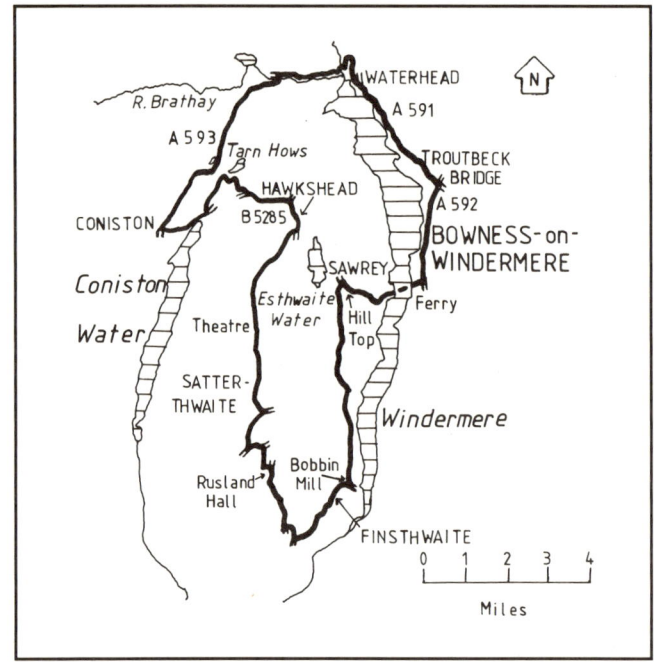

Hawkshead. At the T-junction, turn left and follow the "Coniston" signs. Hawkshead's narrow main street is closed to traffic, but a conveniently situated car park enables one to explore the village on foot.

Everything in the old part of **Hawkshead** seems to be slightly less than full size. Its irregular winding streets, narrow alley ways and quaint cottages combine to give the village a unique atmosphere. It was formerly the centre of a flourishing woollen trade; the outside staircases of some cottages gave access to the rooms which housed the spinning wheels. One such cottage was the home of Ann Tyson, with whom Wordsworth lodged when he was a schoolboy in Hawkshead. Ann Tyson is known to have moved to another cottage at Colthouse on the opposite side of the valley. What is not known for certain is which cottage Wordsworth himself stayed in; perhaps it was both.

Hawkshead village is built round the foot of a glacial knoll, on top of which stands the Parish Church of St. Michael and All Angels. The church is mainly late 15th and early 16th centuries, but the base of the tower is considerably older. Part of the church was rebuilt by Edwin Sandys, Archbishop of York, in 1578. Sandys was born at Esthwaite Hall and also founded the famous Grammar School in 1585. Wordsworth attended the school almost 200 years later. Though no longer used as a school, the building is open to the public from Easter to the end of September. The school received its charter from Queen Elizabeth in 1588, whilst the village received its market charter some 14 years later.

Leave Hawkshead by North Lonsdale Road and continue to follow the "Coniston" signs. Shortly after leaving the village, the road (still B5285) turns left, but one may wish to visit the **Courthouse** just beyond the junction on the B5286. The building is all that remains of the manorial buildings of Hawkshead formerly owned by Furness Abbey. It is owned by the National Trust and is run as a museum of rural life by the Abbot Hall Gallery of Kendal. The field opposite the Courthouse is the site of Hawkshead Show on the first Tuesday in September. One of the principal attractions of this annual event is (and has been annually for over 200 years) an exhibition of local Herdwick sheep.

After ¾-mile, the B5285 leads to Hawkshead Hill, where turn right and follow the "Tarn Hows" signs. The popular beauty spot of **Tarn Hows** (or simply The Tarns) amply justifies its reputation. Its exceptional charm results from an indefinable blend of colours, clouds, mountains, pines and water. My own favourite season is autumn, but the superb backcloth of mountains (which includes Fairfield, Helvellyn, the Langdale Pikes and Coniston Old Man) is breathtakingly beautiful at any time of year. Opponents of reservoir and similar schemes might care to ponder that Tarn Hows is also man-made in that it was created by artificially raising the water level of three smaller pools.

On leaving Tarn Hows there is a spectacular view of Yewdale below on the right, with Lake Coniston (or Coniston Water) ahead. A one-way system enables this beautiful but narrow road to be negotiated in safety. On

Boats by the score on a busy Coniston Water. This view looks north from Coniston Hall.   *(Colin Denwood)*

rejoining the B5285, bear right. The road skirts the edge of the lake at the approach to Coniston village. (If not wishing to explore the village, turn right (signed "Ambleside") and, on meeting the A593, turn right again).

   Coniston village lies in a lovely setting between the lake and the Old Man. The summit of Coniston Old Man (2,635 feet) can be reached by a fairly easy climb. The village also provides a base for serious climbers of the severe faces of Dow Crag (2,555 feet), a little farther west. The Coniston district contains a number of old slate quarries and disused copper mines. Much of the area, including the huge North Coniston estate, is now under the protection of the National Trust. Monk Coniston Hall is let to the Holiday Fellowship.

   John Ruskin is buried in Coniston churchyard. The Ruskin Museum contains many of his personal relics, including his collection of minerals. Part of the museum is devoted to other items of local history, including photographs of Donald Campbell's last (and fatal) attempt to break the world water speed record. Arthur Ransome used the area around Coniston Water as the setting for a number of his books. The Victorian steam yacht *Gondola* has been reconstructed by the National Trust and now sails regularly on the lake.

   Just beyond Coniston church, turn right into the A593 and drive through the sublime scenery of Yewdale. Yew Tree Farm, which stands to the left of the road, features a spinning gallery. On one incredibly beautiful March morning, I spent an hour or so by the picturesque **Yew Tree Tarn,** which lies to the left of the road two miles north of Coniston. The sun shone from a cloudless blue sky, whilst the still tarn reflected the pine trees and snow-capped mountains like a mirror. During the whole of this time, hardly a vehicle passed by on the road.

The road climbs through a low pass before descending into Lower Langdale. Cross the River Brathay at Skelwith Bridge and two miles later cross the River Rothay at Clappersgate. Immediately over the bridge, turn left, then right, to Waterhead. The return to Bowness-on-Windermere is by the now familar lakeside roads: A591 and A592.

<table>
<tr><td>DAY TOUR
FROM
BOWNESS – 5</td><td># Lunesdale, Dentdale and the Lyth Valley</td></tr>
</table>

This route contains majestic countryside, some interesting old towns and two captivating houses, Sizergh Castle and Levens Hall. It is suggested that to do justice to all, the drive should be undertaken as a full-day trip, whilst the houses should be visited on a Wednesday, Thursday or Sunday afternoon as a separate half-day trip (described at the end of the chapter). Sizergh Castle is open from 2 p.m. to 5.45 p.m. on Sundays, Wednesdays and Thursdays; also on Bank Holiday Mondays and all Mondays in August. Levens Hall is open from 11 a.m. to 5 p.m. on Sundays, Tuesdays, Wednesdays and Thursdays; also on Bank Holiday Mondays. (The gardens are open daily). Some of the steam exhibits at Levens are in steam on Sundays and Bank Holiday Mondays, so these are ideal times to undertake the half-day trip. Aim to be at Sizergh for opening time.

THIS tour commences with a visit to the "auld grey town" of Kendal. The River Lune is followed to its source, then a return is made via the Rawthey Valley to middle Lunesdale at Sedbergh. After a detour through Lower Dentdale and Barbondale, we return yet again to Lunesdale and the charming town of Kirkby Lonsdale. Sizergh Castle and Levens Hall, both built round pele towers, lie close together in the Kent Valley, through which we pass briefly before returning to Bowness-on-Windermere via the Lyth Valley.

Leave Bowness by the Kendal road (opposite St. Martin's Church). Follow the A5074 for ¾-mile, then turn left into the B5284 (signed "Kendal 8"), which climbs up past Windermere Golf Club. It is a pleasant, undulating road with views of the Howgills and Pennines ahead, the only community of any significance being the village of Crook. Cross the A591 into the A5284 and shortly enter Kendal.

One must follow the one-way system around what is, in effect, an enormous elongated roundabout. It is worth parking the car and exploring **Kendal** on foot. The River Kent flows through the town and there are attractive riverside paths and gardens. It is crosssed near the southern end of the town by Nether Bridge. Close by is the rectangular parish church of Holy Trinity. With its double aisles, it is extraordinarily wide (over 100 feet) and commodious. Its architecture is complex, the earliest part dating from the 13th century. It was much restored in the mid-19th century. The town is referred to in Domesday Book; a modern interpretation of the entry would be Kirkby Kendal, indicating the existence of an early church, probably on the site of Holy Trinity.

Adjacent to the church is **Abbot Hall.** The hall itself, an 18th century house by Carr of York, contains an art gallery opened in 1962 by Princess Margaret. In addition to paintings, including some by Turner and Romney (who was born in Kendal), the gallery houses a variety of furniture and glass. The stable block contains the Museum of Lakeland Life and Industry, opened in 1971 by Princess Alexandra. This excellent museum won the first National Heritage Museum of the Year award in 1973. It contains a number of rooms furnished in local period style. A wide variety of trades is represented, including farmer, printer, hand-loom weaver, mechanic, wheelwright, quarryman, miner and bobbin-maker. Some adjacent cottages have recently been converted and added to the museum. A joint admission ticket to both the art gallery and the museum is available. The grounds of Abbot Hall are now a public park and provide an attractive open space alongside the river near to the town centre.

The remains of a stronghold on Castle How date back to prehistoric times, whilst the Romans built the fort of Alavna on the banks of the Kent at Watercrook, ½-mile south of the present Nether Bridge. The ruins of Kendal Castle date from the 12th century. The castle was the birthplace of Catherine Parr, herself twice widowed before becoming King Henry VIII's sixth wife. The Castle Dairy, in Wildman Street, is an interesting 14th century house. Close by is the Kendal Museum, with its famous wildlife collection. In Beast Banks, near Castle How, is the Peartree Chapel, which until 1968 was the home of a Society of Inghamites, a tiny denomination of followers of Benjamin Ingham (1712-1772), now concentrated around Colne in Lancashire, though formerly much more widespread. The old brewery, in Highgate, is now an Arts Centre, whilst further along, in Stricklandgate, is the Victorian Town Hall.

Behind the main streets are considerable numbers of old yards and alleys, though many have been demolished. One theory is that these were built to enable the townspeople to hide from marauding Scots, whilst another is that they were built to house communities of the same tradespeople in the days — many centuries, in fact — when wool was a major industry in the town. Kendal's industries to-day include insurance, tourism and shoe manufacturing. The Kendal gathering, a festival-cum-carnival, takes place annually during the fortnight following the August Bank Holiday.

Leave Kendal by the northbound A6 and, after passing under the railway bridge by the station, fork right into the A685. As we begin to climb, the London-Glasgow railway appears on the slopes of Hay Fell to the right. We keep close to the railway for a mile or so as both wind through the Mint Valley. The road crosses the Dales Way footpath at Grayrigg Foot, then passes through **Grayrigg** village. Grayrigg Tarn lies to the left a mile beyond the village.

Beyond the junction with the B6257, which comes up the Lune Valley through Beckfoot, the road descends into the **Lune Gorge,** or Tebay Gorge. There is a small car park to the right of the road near the foot of the hill, provided by the Rees-Jeffreys Road Fund, from which there is a spectacular view of the River Lune, the West Coast main line railway and the M6 motorway as they thread their way through the narrow gorge with the Howgill Fells beyond. A large stone commemorates a Civic Trust award for the landscaping of the Lancaster-Penrith section of the motorway. The 3-acre site of a Roman fort stands at **Low Borrow Bridge** close to the confluence of the River Lune and the Borrow Beck, which comes down the secluded Borrowdale (not to be confused with the Keswick Borrowdale) to the left. The fort stood on the main Roman road north to Carlisle.

Eventually cross over the motorway, railway and river, in this highly congested section of the Lune Gorge, to the village of **Tebay.** This was formerly an important railway junction and town. Some of the houses served as overnight hostels for engine drivers. Tebay's engine sheds housed about thirty locomotives. With the closure of the Kirkby Stephen branch and the electrification of the main line, thus eliminating the need for banking engines (to push trains up the bank from the rear), between 100 and 200 families moved out of Tebay, so that it became an almost deserted town. At the end of the village street, keep left, then, at the roundabout, turn right (still A685, signed "Brough").

The road now follows the trackbed of the former Tebay-Kirkby Stephen railway for several miles, still following the valley of the River Lune, whereas the motorway and railway climb over Shap Fell. The village of **Newbiggin-on-Lune** stands near to the source of the river, which is formed from numerous becks flowing down from Ravenstonedale Common. Skirt the edge of Newbiggin and, ¾-mile later, turn right (signed "Ravenstonedale"). At **Ravenstonedale,** an ancient Norse community, turn right by St. Oswald's Church and follow the Sedbergh signs. The church is 18th century in appearance, but parts of it are much older. It has box pews, arranged College-style, and a three-decker pulpit.

On meeting the A683, turn right by the remote Fat Lamb Guest House. The road follows the valley of the River Rawthey through the Howgills. At Rawthey Bridge, with its medieval stone heads overlooking the river, we enter the Yorkshire Dales National Park, though remaining in Cumbria. The Cross Keys Temperance Hotel, which stands to the right of the road, was built around 1600 and was substantially altered in the 18th and 19th centuries. It was given to the National Trust in 1949.

From the hotel, a footpath leads to the series of cascades which comprise **Cautley Spout** Waterfall. This can be seen from a small lay-by to the left of the road shortly beyond the Cross Keys, but this view gives no impression of

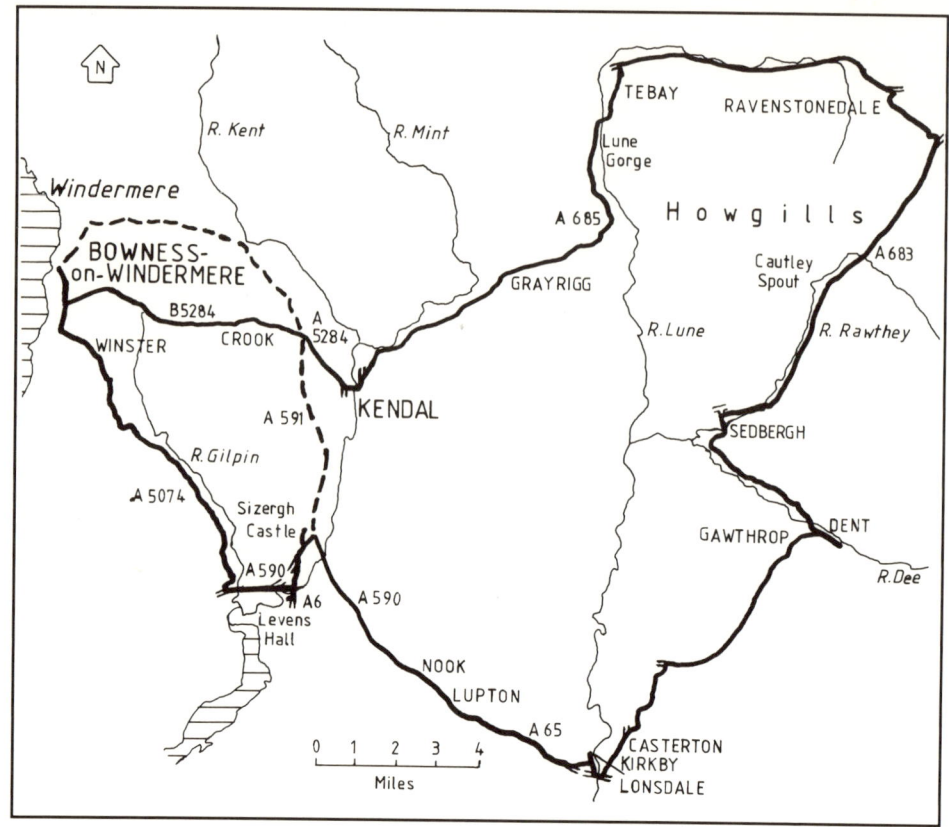

the real size of the waterfall, which needs to be approached on foot to be appreciated. To the left of the Spout are the massive Cautley Crags, which stand on the slopes of The Calf (2,200 feet), the highest point in the Howgills. Ravens nest in these mountains, which, in view of their smooth, rounded contours, have been likened to sleeping elephants.

In a side valley to the left of the road stands the ancient Hebblethwaite Hall, close to which was a former woollen mill. The Rawthey valley once had both flourishing woollen and cotton trades. Its only town, **Sedbergh,** is today probably best known for its school, which was founded in 1525. Bear left on entering the town to follow the one-way system and at the T-junction by St. Andrew's church, turn left.

From Sedbergh, follow the "Dent" signs. The road soon crosses a narrow bridge over the River Rawthey and winds past the village of Millthrop, then round the edge of Long Rigg, which separates the Rawthey and Dee valleys. We are now in charming **Dentdale;** the dale takes its name from its "town" rather than its river. The Dales Way follows the river on the opposite bank to the road. At Barth Bridge, 4½ miles from Sedbergh, the road bends right to

40

cross the River Dee and, one mile later, enters Dent. A car park and picnic area stands to the left of the road at the entrance to the village, which should be explored on foot.

Dent has an air of timelessness, enhanced by its cobbled main street. Many years ago, I met a 45-year old resident who had been no further than Sedbergh in his life and was both excited and frightened at the prospect of a possible forthcoming visit to Carlisle. However, on a more recent visit, a glance at the notice board in the church porch indicated that the meetings of a regular discussion group had been re-timed to enable members to see the end of a popular television programme before attending. The church was founded in Norman times, was rebuilt in 1417 and restored in 1590, 1787 (when the tower was rebuilt) and 1889. It contains some good 17th century woodwork with box pews round the sides. The chancel floor is of local Dent marble.

Dent and Sedbergh were formerly part of the extensive West Riding of Yorkshire. At one time, they were centres of a hand-knitting industry, which had a prolific output. Dent's most famous son, Adam Sedgwick, who became Professor of Geology at Cambridge, is commemorated by a fountain made from a large block of Shap granite. In 1985, a series of events in Dent and Sedbergh marked the bicentenary of his birth. Guided walking tours of the village take place on certain days of the week starting from the George and Dragon Hotel. There are delightful riverside walks in both directions from Dent.

Leave Dent by the way we entered, as all other exits lead to North Yorkshire. After ¾-mile, fork left into a narrow lane (signed "Gawthrop ¼; Barbon 6"). The next mile or so calls for great care on the part of the driver. At the ancient village of Gawthrop, turn left after crossing Haycote Bridge. The road quickly leaves Dentdale behind as it climbs up Peas Gill. The sweeping sides of Barkin Fell appear to the right of the road. The summit, Calf Top (1,999 feet) fails to reach mountain status by one foot.

We are now in lonely **Barbondale,** a little known corner of Cumbria. The road through the dale has been surfaced in recent years and passing places provided. At Short Gill Bridge, the road leaves the Yorkshire Dales National Park. The Barkin Beck runs to the right as one descends. The valley becomes less desolate and more wooded in its lower reaches. Take the left-hand fork, signed "Casterton", on the return to the Lune valley. The road runs along the side of the valley, which lies below on the right.

At the approach to Casterton, we leave the open moorland behind and enter wooded country followed by agricultural countryside. Turn right over the trackbed of the former Clapham-Lowgill railway, then immediately turn left and, on rejoining the A683, turn left into **Casterton.** The village lies close to the Roman road from Ribchester to Carlisle. Casterton School moved here in 1833 from Cowan Bridge, where it was founded ten years earlier for the daughters of clergymen and was attended by the Bronte sisters. Holy Trinity church, Casterton, was built in 1831-33 by the founder of the school, Revd. W. Carus Wilson. The short chancel was added later. Casterton Hall, one of several large houses in this part of Lonsdale (Lunesdale), stands on the right of the road just beyond the village.

One mile beyond Casterton, **Devil's Bridge** stands on the right, immediately before the junction with the A65. This graceful, medieval bridge, which spans a lovely stretch of the River Lune, is now a footbridge. Free car parking is provided on both sides of the bridge at this popular spot. The pool below the bridge is a favourite among salmon fishermen (with permits!). A public footpath runs from the far side of the bridge along the riverside to Kirkby Lonsdale town and Ruskin's View. Cross the river by turning right into the A65 and using the "new" Stanley Bridge, opened in 1932. Then take the second turning right into the B6254 into Kirkby Lonsdale unless, of course, one has already visited the town on foot via Devil's Bridge.

Kirkby Lonsdale is a delightful old town. Half way along Main Street is the Market Square, a colourful and busy spot on Thursdays. The square was laid out in its present form in the early 19th century, when the Royal Hotel and the Trustee Savings Bank were built, but the Butter Cross is relatively modern (1905). The ancient market cross, which formerly stood near the junction of Main Street and Market Street, has been re-erected in Swinemarket, close to Horsemarket. The many other features of interest in the town include the Elizabethan Manor House in Mill Brow, the Sun Hotel and the remains of a motte and bailey castle at Cockpit Hill, near the Vicarage.

Kirkby Lonsdale's most interesting building is the Norman church, built on the site of an even earlier building, and approached from the far end of Main Street. Like many churches, its architectural history is complex, with signs of incompleted plans. We should note especially the three Norman pillars and arches. Through the churchyard is a gazebo, beyond which is the famous **Ruskin's View,** immortalised by Turner. Ruskin's own description of the view — "one of the loveliest scenes in England and therefore the world" — is equally well-known. Barbondale can be seen as a fold in the hills beyond the Lune. Kirkby Lonsdale was the Lowton of Charlotte Bronte's *Jane Eyre*. The local Civic Society has produced a picture-map and walking-tour route giving a one-mile "trail" of the town.

Leave Kirkby Lonsdale by Mitchelgate, a narrow turning off Market Street near to the church. This runs into the B6446, which should be followed as it bears to the right. On meeting the A65, turn right. Near Lupton the Lake District fells re-appear ahead. The village of **Lupton** boasts several fine old houses and farms, mostly near the main road, incuding Foulstone Farm and Lupton Tower. One mile beyond Nook, keep straight ahead at the two roundabouts into the A590. Three miles later, turn left (signed "Barrow A590") * and almost immediately turn right to Sizergh Castle.

Sizergh Castle has been the main residence of the Strickland family from

* If time is pressing, continue along the A591 to Windermere.

1239 to the present date. It was given to the National Trust by the Hornyold-Stricklands in 1950. The oldest part of the present building is the pele tower, which dates from c.1340. This was one of a series of castles and fortified towers built to provide shelter and security during the battles between the English and the Scots over the border country prior to 1603. It is approximately 60 feet high, 60 feet wide and 40 feet deep, whilst its walls taper from 9½ feet thick at the bottom to 5½ feet at the top. Adjoining the tower is a Tudor Great Hall and Elizabethan central block, with two Elizabethan wings.

The castle is surprisingly large inside considering its compact exterior. It contains some particularly fine Elizabethan panelling and a number of elaborate 16th century chimney pieces. Amongst the items of furniture are some unique Stuart and Jacobean relics. Catherine Parr is said to have stayed at Sizergh after the death of Henry VIII; her aunt was the wife of Sir Thomas Strickland. The grounds and gardens are attractively laid out, especially on the south-east side of the castle, and contain evidence of a former moat.

Return from Sizergh by the way we entered past the Strickland Arms. On meeting the A590, turn right, then fork left (signed "A6 Milnthorpe"). Levens Deer Park lies to the left of the A6, which before the opening of the M6 motorway was the main north-south road through Cumbria. Three-quarters of a mile after joining the A6, we come to Levens Bridge. To visit Levens Hall, keep straight on at the traffic lights, then after crossing the bridge, turn right into the grounds of the hall.

Levens Hall is the largest Elizabethan hall in Cumbria. It is particularly well-known for its gardens, which were laid out by the Frenchman, Guillaume Beaumont, in the last decade of the 17th century. These are probably the finest topiary gardens in England. The original plans for the gardens have been carefully preserved and followed, though many of the trees have grown out of all proportion to the original intentions. The yew trees and box trees have been clipped to fantastic shapes. The 100 acres of parkland contain dark brown (known as "black") deer.

The hall was once owned by the Redmans, later by the Bellinghams, then (in the late 17th century) by the Grahams, ancestors of the present owners, the Bagots. It dates from the 13th century and, like Sizergh, was built round a pele tower. It contains some fine plaster-work, especially in the ceilings and chimney pieces. Paintings include works by Rubens and Lely, whilst the Spanish leather wall hangings are notable. The furniture includes some fine Charles II pieces and both old and modern harpsichords. The hall has a splendid collection of steam engines, depicting the development of steam power. A number of traction engines, including the large *Bertha* and the small *Little Gem,* are in steam on Sundays and Bank Holiday Mondays. There is a restaurant, cafeteria, gift shop and plant centre.

On leaving the grounds, turn left to re-cross the River Kent, then immediately turn left again. The road now runs into the A590 (signed "Barrow"). Whitbarrow Scar dominates the view ahead as we travel along the causeway across the estuary of the Rivers Kent and Gilpin. One mile after joining the dual carriageway road, turn right into the A5074 (signed "Bowness"). Immediately beyond the Gilpin Bridge Inn, turn left (still A5074) and return into the Lake District National Park. The valley of the Gilpin is known locally as the **Lyth Valley.** It is particularly colourful in the spring with daffodils and (for a short time) damson blossom and is popular in the damson season. Follow the A5074 through the Lyth Valley and the village of Winster back to Bowness-on-Windermere.

Suggested separate half-day trip to Sizergh Castle and Levens Hall

Leave Bowness by the Windermere road (A5074). At Windermere Town, turn right into the A591. A small detour can be made into the village of Ings (to the right of the A591) with its Georgian church. Follow the A591 through Staveley and along the Kendal by-pass as far as the junction with the A590 (signed "Barrow"). From here, proceed as above to Sizergh Castle, then to Levens Hall and return via the Lyth Valley.

<table>
<tr><td>LINK
ROUTE</td><td></td></tr>
</table>

Bowness-on-Windermere to Keswick

THE route from Bowness-on-Windermere to Keswick is short but full of interest. It follows the busy main artery of the Lake District — A591 — but a short detour into Grasmere village is recommended. Those towing caravans might wish to keep to the A591, which by-passes Grasmere.

The section from Bowness to Ambleside is described in the opening part of Day Tour 3 (page 25). Follow Windermere past the National Park Centre at Brockhole to Waterhead. From Ambleside to Keswick the route is as given in the latter part of Chapter 4 — Day Tour 4 (page 65). This leads through the "Lake Poets' Country" close to Wordsworth's homes at Rydal Mount and Dove Cottage, then over Dunmail Raise and alongside Thirlmere to Keswick.

4. Central Cumbria

Keswick is easily accessible from the M6 Motorway: leave at Junction 40, then take the A66 westwards.
The nearest railway station is Penrith.

FOR our purposes, Central Cumbria comprises the area which extends northwards from Ambleside as far as Cockermouth and eastwards from the coast to the Eamont/Eden. The only major part to be excluded is the industrialised coastal region around Workington and Whitehaven.

The area is based on the "Borrowdale Volcanics" — the rocks which give Central Cumbria its distinctive craggy appearance. To the north lie the ancient Skiddaw slates. It is an area essentially for the walker and climber. The motorist merely scratches the surface and is completely unable to penetrate a large part of Central Cumbria. Such routes as exist mainly circumnavigate the central mountain core and it is difficult to avoid some repetition.

My first holiday in Central Cumbria was with a school party which stayed at Keswick Youth Hostel one Easter — an ideal time for a walking holiday. Many memories remain: Saddleback; Catbells; sailing on Derwentwater; the climb up Helvellyn and the spectacular walks along Striding Edge and Swirral Edge; the hike over Styhead Pass in heavy cloud and the descent to Wasdale in sunshine.

Keswick

BEAUTIFULLY situated near the northern end of Derwentwater and surrounded by mountains is our chosen centre for touring Central Cumbria: Keswick. The town is dominated to the north by Skiddaw and Blencathra (Saddleback). The River Greta flows through Keswick from the east before it joins the River Derwent just beyond the point where the latter leaves Derwentwater. The enlarged river then flows north-westwards into Bassenthwaite.

Despite the building of the A66 by-pass, Keswick is a busy, congested town with narrow streets. Standing in the main street is the Moot Hall, built on the site of a courthouse dating back to 1571. It is said to have been built from stones brought from the former mansion of the Earls of Derwentwater on Lord's Island — one of several islands in the lake. Built in 1813 and restored in 1971, the Moot Hall has a church-like appearance, with its tower and one-handed clock. The ground-floor arches were formerly open-sided and housed a small market. The Moot Hall is now the local Information Centre; guided walks start from here.

Keswick is not a particularly old town. The original settlement was at Great Crosthwaite, half-a-mile to the north-west, where the parish church of St. Kentigern still stands; the poet Southey is buried in the churchyard. St. John's church, with its prominent spire, was built in 1838; Hugh Walpole is buried in its churchyard.

Copper and lead have been mined in the Keswick area since the 15th century. The industry reached its height in the reign of Elizabeth I. German labour was imported and forests were felled to make charcoal for smelting. The smelting works were destroyed in the Civil War. Also in the reign of Elizabeth I, graphite was discovered in Borrowdale; this led to the development of pencil making in Keswick. Today the Cumberland Pencil Company — the oldest in the world — uses imported graphite. The well-laid out museum and exhibition centre at the company's Southey Works in Keswick is open daily in summer. Nearby is the School of Industrial Arts founded by Canon and Mrs. Rawnsley for local unemployed men.

Keswick first became well-known following the writings of the Lake Poets. Coleridge moved into Greta Hall in 1800, to be joined three years later by Southey. (Mrs Coleridge and Mrs Southey were sisters). Shelley honeymooned in Keswick, whilst the Wordsworths, Sir Walter Scott, Charles Lamb, de Quincey, Keats, Tennyson and Robert Louis Stevenson all visited the town.

Fitz Park Museum contains a valuable collection of manuscripts by Wordsworth, Coleridge, Southey and Walpole. It also houses an extensive collection of minerals and fossils, including a rock harmonium and an 1834 relief model of the Lake District. The park itself contains a large variety of species of trees, as well as tennis courts, bowling greens and putting greens. International sheepdog trials are held here annually in May.

There is a miniature golf course at Hope Park alongside the road from the town centre to the lake. From the landing stage, launches sail round Derwentwater, calling it several points en route; the complete circuit takes 50 minutes. A short walk from Keswick landing stage leads to Friar's Crag, one of the best-known and oft-photographed spots in the Lake District. Friar's Crag and Calf Close Bay were bought by public subscription in 1922 and given to the National Trust in memory of Canon Rawnsley, Vicar of Keswick and one of the founders of the Trust.

In the lakeside car park, close to the landing stage, stands the Century Theatre, home of Theatre North. Originally a travelling theatre, at the time of writing there are proposals to move the theatre to a permanent home in the former Keswick railway station. At present, the station (which opened in 1865, closed in 1972 and originally housed the head offices of the Cockermouth, Keswick and Penrith Railway) contains a small railway museum.

Keswick — capital of central Cumbria. In the middle of the picture is the 16th century Moot Hall, now an information centre. *(Jack Wetherby)*

Every July, thousands of pilgrims invade Keswick for the annual Convention. Numerous camps spring up in the area to house the visitors to this inter-denominational Christian festival. The Keswick Agricultural Society holds its annual one-day show in August.

As at Kendal, many cottages and yards close to Keswick town centre have been demolished. In recent years, the road system has been considerably altered and large car parks have been created. Although this provision has been made for the ever-increasing number of motorists visiting the town, Keswick is still essentially a centre for the walker, with the many alluring peaks close by. The less energetic can appreciate the modest height of Castle Head (529 feet) whilst even better views can be enjoyed from Latrigg (1,203 feet). Whether a walker or a motorist (or both), the visitor will find Keswick to be an ideal centre.

Whinlatter and Honister Passes

Wordsworth House, Cockermouth is closed on Thursdays, whilst Wythop Mill, near Embleton, is closed on Mondays.

THE outward journey is via the relatively easy Whinlatter Pass, with its interesting Visitor Centre. The only place of any size to be visited is Cockermouth, best known as the birthplace of William and Dorothy Wordsworth. The return is via the Vale of Lorton, the spectacular Honister Pass and the lovely valley of Borrowdale.

Leave Keswick by Main Street and the inappropriately named High Hill. At the time of writing, the road north-west from Keswick is numbered B5289. However, this is the third different number which it has borne in recent years, the previous ones being A66 and, before that, A594. (With the opening of the Keswick by-pass, one might have expected that the northbound road would be numbered A5271, a more logical and appropriate number for such a good road, and that Crosthwaite Road would be B5289).

It is worth digressing a little from the road to look at **Crosthwaite church.** Where the main road sweeps round to the left on leaving Keswick town, a lane leads off to the right to the church. Sometimes known as "the Cathedral of the Lakes", the church was founded by St. Kentigern in A.D. 553. The present church is mainly late Perpendicular (early 16th century), but the north chapel dates from c.1340. The church was restored and re-roofed in 1844-45 and in 1909 part of the south aisle was converted into a baptistry in recognition of twenty-five years of work in the parish by Canon H. D. Rawnsley, who was also one of the three founder members of the National Trust. The church contains several monuments, including a marble effigy of the poet Robert Southey by the self-taught J. G. Lough. Southey's grave was restored by the Brazilian Government in 1961. (The poet wrote a history of Brazil).

Rejoin the B5289 and after ½-mile turn left into the A66. After a further mile, fork left into the B5292 (signed "Whinlatter Pass") and immediately enter **Braithwaite** village. Follow the narrow road past the Royal Oak Inn, then climb steeply up through Thornthwaite Forest. There is a magnificent view over Bassenthwaite Lake and Skiddaw from a conveniently situated car park on the right of the road, adjacent to the Forestry Commission's **Brows Wood picnic area.**

Whinlatter Pass climbs to a height of 1,043 feet between Grisedale Pike and Lord's Seat. At the summit is the **Whinlatter Pass Visitor Centre** (admission free). This tells the story of the lakeland forests, and in particular

Thornthwaite Forest, with a slide-tape presentation and other displays. From the summit, the road descends at 12% through woods to the Vale of Lorton.

Continue to follow the B5292* through the verdant vale to Cockermouth. Pass under the A66 to enter the town, then turn left into Victoria Road and right into Station Road, following the "Town Centre" signs. **Cockermouth** has an attractive tree-lined main street in which stands a statue of the sixth Earl of Mayo, a former M.P. for Cockermouth and Viceroy of India. The local writer, J. B. Bradbury, has written a booklet (available in local shops and at the Information Centre) describing a town trail.

Cockermouth is a historic town situated at the point where the River Cocker runs into the River Derwent. Cockermouth Castle incorporates some stone from the Roman camp of Derventio at Papcastle, a mile from the town. Located between the two rivers, the castle played a major part in the numerous border struggles from the 12th to the 16th centuries and was largely dismantled after the Civil War. Cockermouth market dates from 1226, whilst the town became a borough in 1295. It is now an important tourist and agriculural centre.

The town is best known as the birthplace of William and Dorothy Wordsworth and their three brothers. **Wordsworth House,** in Main Street, was built in 1745 and is now in the possession of the National Trust. William was born here in 1770 and spent his formative years in these graceful surroundings. Several rooms, including the drawing room and the morning room, are furnished in the style of the 18th century. The terrace walk at the rear of the house is referred to in *The Prelude* and is also open to the public (via the house).

Leave Cockermouth via Castlegate, which runs from the eastern end of Main Street (signed "Keswick"). Pass through the village of **Embleton,** then, just beyond the Wheatsheaf Inn, turn right (signed "Wythop ½") and cross the A66. **Wythop Mill,** which stands to the right of the road in Wythop village, is open to the public. It is an interesting example of a small, historic mill with working water-wheel. Part of the mill has been converted into an attractive cafe.

On leaving the mill, turn right (signed "Lorton") and cross the stream, noting the collection of implements in the garden of the house opposite at the cross-roads. Our road now runs along the foot of Ling Fell. Keep straight ahead at each successive junction and cross the B5292 (our road being signed "Eaglesfield 3"). Cross over the River Cocker at Southwaite Mill, then at the next T-junction, turn left (signed "Rogerscale 1").

The Lakeland fells begin to close in again along the road to Rogerscale. At the next T-junction, turn left to cross back over the River Cocker and into the village of **Low Lorton,** where turn right into the B5289 (signed "Buttermere 6"). Lorton Hall is a 17th century building constructed round an ancient pele look-out tower and set in attractive gardens.

* The route can be shortened by turning left at High Lorton and following the "Buttermere" signs, thus omitting Cockermouth and Wythop.

Continue to follow the "Buttermere" signs, bearing left into a narrow lane (still B5289) two miles south of Lorton. Beyond Lanthwaite, descend to **Crummock Water,** home of the char fish. It is possible to walk right round the lake, thereby appreciating to the full its sublime setting. Scale Force, a 100-foot waterfall (the highest in the Lake District), can be approached from the far side of the lake.

The road is especially attractive beyond Rannerdale Farm. The view towards High Crag, with the trees along the sandy shore of the lake in the foreground, is a favourite among artists. The scene is reminiscent of a mini-Alpine one as the road rounds Buttermere Hause, clinging to the ledge above the water's edge, with the mountains towering around us.

Buttermere village occupies the small neck of flat land which separates Crummock water from Buttermere lake and forms the delta of the Sail Beck. Sour Milk Gill descends from Red Pike opposite the village, which is surrounded by mountains formed of rocks over 500,000,000 years old. Keep to the B5289, which runs close to the lake. The road climbs through the glaciated Gatesgarthdale to the Honister Pass, with the scree-covered slopes of Yew Crag on the left and Honister Crag on the right.

Honister Pass lies between Dale Head and Fleetwith Pike. The B5289 climbs at 25% to the summit, which, despite its dramatic surroundings is less than 1,200 feet above sea level. The slate quarries to the right of our road are

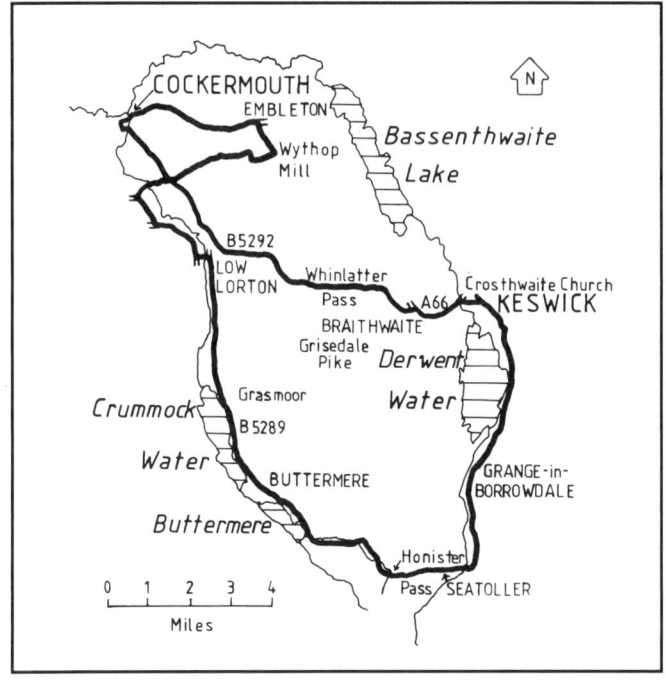

still working, but the former graphite and plumbago mines, which formed the basis of the Keswick pencil industry in the 17th and 18th centuries, have long since closed. The descent — 20% at first, steepening to 25% — reminds one of the Rest-and-be-thankful Pass (Strathclyde) with its similar fine views.

The hamlet of **Seatoller** nestles at the foot of Honister Pass. It was largely built by the quarry owners for their workmen. The road to the right leads to Seathwaite, beyond which paths lead through the heart of the Lake District via Styhead Tarn and Pass to Wasdale and via Angle Tarn and Rossett Gill to Langdale. Seatoller Barn Interpretative Centre forms a base for exploring the vicinity. Guided walks of varying length start from here, as does the 2½-mile long Johnny Wood nature trail, laid out by the Lake District Naturalists' Trust and including a superb viewpoint (927 feet high) over Borrowdale.

The upper part of **Borrowdale** is quite open and lush, but beyond **Rosthwaite,** with its narrow street, we pass through the "Jaws of Borrowdale", where the dale squeezes between Eel Crags to the left and Grange Fell to the right, whilst Castle Crag stands between the jaws in the centre of the dale to the left. From its summit, crowned by an ancient fort, fine views of Derwentwater can be enjoyed. The road is forced to cling close to the banks of the River Derwent through the constricted part of the valley.

Some 1½ miles beyond Rosthwaite, near the quarries at the foot of Grange Fell, a footpath leads to the **Bowder Stone.** The roadside lay-by is reserved for coaches, but a free car park off the road has been provided by the National Trust. The Bowder Stone is a huge boulder, estimated to weigh nearly 2,000 tons, poised on a tiny base. Its 36-feet high summit can be reached by means of 29 wooden steps.

A double-arched bridge leads off to our left to **Grange,** the largest hamlet in Borrowdale; its houses are gathered round an open space. Keep to the B5289, which leads past the Lodore Hotel, behind which a footpath leads to the **Lodore Falls.** The falls are best seen after heavy rain; otherwise they can be disappointing if one expects them to accord to Southey's famous description.

The drive through Borrowdale contains all the ingredients of Lake District secenery: lake, woods, mountains, waterfalls, narrow roads and National Trust property all around! Follow the eastern shore of **Derwentwater** back to Keswick. The lake is one of the widest in the Lake District and is dotted with small islands. There are views of Catbells on the opposite side of the lake, whilst the road to the oft-photographed Ashness Bridge and Watendlath leads off to the right. Turn left at the first roundabout, then keep straight on at the next roundabout to return to Keswick town centre.

Landscape of northern Lakeland. Jacob sheep and a farmhouse near Loweswater complement the mountain backcloth of Grasmoor. *(Ivor Nicholas)*

West of Eden —
Penrith and Dalemain

Dalemain is closed on Friday and Saturday and Penrith Steam Museum is closed on Saturday, but both are open on the Saturday of Bank Holiday weekends. Brougham Castle is open daily.

THIS tour links a number of historic sites dating from 1500 B.C. to the present century. We call at a Bronze Age megalithic circle, pass an iron age hill fort, explore a historic town, see two ruined castles, pass the sites of a Roman fort and two ancient henges, visit a house dating from medieval, Tudor and early Georgian times and finally call at an old village with a church built on the site of an ancient monastery and a splendidly preserved pele tower.

Leave Keswick by the A5271 Penrith road. After one mile, bear left into the A591, then immediately fork right (signed "Castlerigg Stone Circle") and climb up a narrow road. The 3,500 year old **Megalithic circle** stands in a field to the right of the road at the top of the hill. It is approximately 100 feet in diameter and consists of 38 large stones with a further 10 stones within it forming a rectangle at the south-east end. It was probably used for religious ceremonies and is also known as "Druids' Circle". There is a fine view down St. John's Vale from Castlerigg Circle.

At the T-junction at the foot of the ensuing hill, turn right into the original Keswick-Penrith road, then, at the next T-junction, turn right again into the newer Keswick-Penrith road. After a further mile, turn right again into the present-day Keswick-Penrith road (A66). This road by-passes the village of Threlkeld, nestling under the foot of Blencathra (Saddleback), and the hamlet of Scales.

Leave the fast A66 almost four miles after joining it by taking a left turn (signed "Mungrisdale 2"). Saddleback stands to the left as we enter the Mungrisdale valley but soon disappears from sight behind Souther Fell. At the entrance to **Mungrisdale** village, the River Glenderamackin runs below on the left. The narrow road winds through the village, passing the small white 18th century church of St. Kentigern, with its three-decker pulpit and box pews, on the right.

On leaving Mungrisdale, fork right (signed "Hutton Roof 2½"). The edge of the Lake District is particularly clearly defined here. Bowscale Fell (2,306 feet) and Carrock Fell (2,174 feet) stand to the left, separated by the valley through which the infant River Caldew runs, whilst less mountainous countryside stretches across to Inglewood Forest on the right. A 5-acre Iron Age hill fort stands on the summit of Carrock Fell.

Go over the cross-roads 1¼ miles north-east of Mungrisdale into a leafy lane (signed "Newsham 2¾") along the edge of Greystoke Forest. This

53

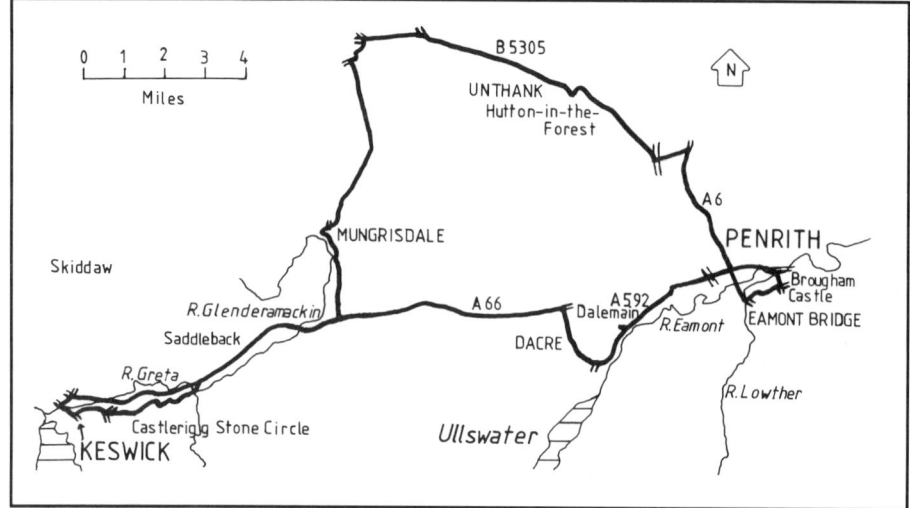

road marks the boundary of the Lake District National Park. At the T-junction five miles from Mungrisdale, turn right (signed "Penrith 12") and, at the next cross-roads, turn right again (signed "Penrith 11").* On meeting the B5303, turn right yet again (signed "Penrith 10").

Follow the fast straight road through the village of Unthank, then sharp left to Hutton-in-the-Forest. After a right-hand corner, **Hutton-in-the-Forest** comes into view to the right. The house and formal gardens are open to the public on certain afternoons. A further straight, wooded stretch of road follows. Cross over the M6 motorway, following the "Penrith (A6)" signs and, at the next roundabout, turn right into the A6. There is a good view towards the Lake District fells to the right on the approach to Penrith.

Parking in Penrith is relatively easy. Like Carlisle, **Penrith** suffered much from border raids. The town contains large open spaces, which were used to protect people and cattle from invasion. The streets and gates were narrow to make defence of the town easier. Penrith was burned down on at least three separate occasions in the 14th century.

Penrith Beacon, a 937-feet high landmark, overlooks the town from the north-east. For centuries, a beacon on this site was used for the lighting of fires to warn of national crises, including the 1588 Armada threat. The present tower was erected in 1719 adjacent to the beacon to provide a shelter for the men who kept watch. It now serves as a viewpoint.

In contrast to Carlisle, Penrith's castle is in ruins and relatively little of it remains; part of the grounds have been landscaped to form a public park, the railway station having been constructed on the rest of the site. Originally built by Bishop Strickland in the late 14th century, the castle was extended in

* Less than ¼-mile later, a road to the right (signed "Lamonby 2¾") leads to Castle Sowerby church, yet another dedicated to St. Kentigern, dating from the 13th century.

the following century. Substantial additions were made by the Nevilles and Richard, Duke of Gloucester (later Richard III), who built a 50-foot long banqueting hall.

Richard lodged at Dockray Hall, now the Gloucester Arms Inn. The Two Lions Inn nearby was also a former mansion of the Lowther family. Robinson's School in Middlegate dates from 1670. The Grammar School, which dates from 1340, moved into its present buildings in 1915. The Town Hall and Public Library were converted from two former Adam-style houses. Several old houses were the town houses of important county families.

St. Andrew's church dates back many centuries, but was rebuilt in 1720 and is a fine example of a classical Georgian church. The lower part of the walls of the tower, which was built by the Nevilles, are several feet thick. The churchyard contains some ancient tombstones, including the so-called "Giant's Grave", which consists of two pre-Norman crosses separated by four hog-back tombstones. It was once thought to be the grave of Owen, King of Cumbria in the 10th century.

Wordsworth's mother and his wife's parents are buried in St. Andrew's churchyard, whilst a small house overlooking the churchyard is said to have been a school attended by the poet. The town contains a number of places of worship. The United Reformed church (which dates from the 1860s) in Duke Street and the Methodist church (which dates from the 1870s) at the corner of Drovers Lane and Wordsworth Sreet are typical of many throughout the country built in the same period, but appear more attractive becuase of the local red sandstone.

Penrith serves as an agricultural and market centre for a wide area. Its market charter dates from 1222. The medieval open spaces, such as Great Dockray, provide useful sites for present day market stalls on Tuesdays and Saturdays. The town is a popular shopping centre, with small-scale shops — a tradition continued in the "Poet's Walk", built on the site of the former Fish Hotel, which was demolished in 1972. Castlegate Foundry, formerly owned by Stalkers, a firm of agricultural engineers, is now a fascinating museum (Penrith Steam Museum) with engines in steam on most days.

Penrith has associations with Anthony Trollope and Samuel Plimsoll, both of whose families lived in the town. It was formerly an important railway junction, but only the north-south line now remains. The main through roads — M6 north-south and A66 east-west — now by-pass Penrith.

Leave Penrith by King Sreet (signed "A6 Shap"), which runs south from the clock tower. At the roundabout ½-mile later, take the second exit (signed "A66 Brough").* Three-quarters of a mile later, turn right (signed "Brougham ½"). The red sandstone **Brougham Castle** stands across the River Eamont. (There is a car park for the castle to the left of the road after crossing the bridge). The 12th century castle was restored in 1651-52 by Lady

* If time is pressing, turn right at this roundabout (signed "A66 Keswick"), then proceed to the A592 (signed "Ullswater"), as later.

55

Anne Clifford, who died here in 1676. It is now in the care of the Department of the Environment.

At the next cross-roads, turn right. The field on the right, between this cross-roads and the castle, was the site of the Roman fort and supply depot of **Brocavum.** The fort stood at the junction of the Roman roads from Ambleside, Carlisle and Catterick. During alterations to the A66 in 1967, a Roman cemetery containing over 200 graves was uncovered.

At the next junction, bear right (signed "Ullswater"). The gateway to Brougham Hall stands straight ahead of us; our road turns to the right, with **Brougham Chapel** on the right connected to the hall by means of a footbridge. The church is rich in woodwork, including both English and Flemish medieval carvings. The 15th century reredos, which formerly occupied the east wall, is now in the Victoria and Albert Museum, London.

On meeting the A6, turn right (signed "Penrith") and cross the bridge over the River Lowther to enter the village of **Eamont Bridge.** The circular Neolithic monument known as **King Arthur's Round Table** stands in a field to the left of the road just before the junction with the B5320. Follow the A6 through Eamont Bridge and, on crossing the bridge which gives the village its name, a second large Neolithic monument, **Mayburgh Henge,** can be seen across the field to the left.

At the roundabout, turn left into the A66 and at the next roundabout (over the M6) keep straight ahead. At the next roundabout again, bear left into the A592 (signed "Ullswater"). Our road now descends into the Eamont valley. The Dalemain estates stand to the right of the road; the house is approached by a short drive which leads off to the right.

Dalemain is an excellent example of a historic home open to the public. It has been in the possession of the Hasell family since 1679. The house itself dates from three distinct periods: the Norman pele tower, the base of which now houses the Yeomanry Museum; the Elizabethan manor-house, which includes the so-called "Fretwork Room" and the "Old Oak Room"; and the early Georgian front, which dates from the 1740s. The entrance hall, Chinese drawing room (with its handpainted wallpaper), drawing room and dining room all contain fine portraits and period furniture. The dining room contains a magnificent silver centre piece presented to Edward Hasell by the shareholders of the Lancaster and Carlisle Railway Company, of which he was chairman. Other rooms on view to the public include the Print Room, the Nursery and the Housekeeper's Room with its hidden priest's hole.

Home-made teas are served in the medieval old hall. The courtyard contains a countryside museum (at the top of a stone staircase) and a museum for fell ponies and agricultural implements (in the Great Barn). There is a picnic area, a children's adventure playground and a two-storey shop. The extensive grounds contain a herd of deer.

The gardens include an attractive terrace, which leads to the Knott garden. A gateway leads from the far end of the higher section of this garden into Lobb's Wood, which provides unexpectedly fine vantage points over Dacre Beck. It is possible to descend from here to the riverside low garden and so back to the terrace. The gardens are noted for their rare trees and unusual plants and reflect the keen interest shown in them by the owner, Mrs. Sylvia McCosh (nee Hasell), authoress of the book *Between Two Gardens*. The whole property and estate is immaculately maintained.

On leaving Dalemain, turn right into the A592 and run alongside the River Eamont. Take the first turning right (signed "Dacre 1"). **Dacre** village lies in a secluded valley. As we descend (at 12%), Dacre castle can be seen opposite. The castle is a particularly well-preserved example of a 14th century crenellated pele tower. The Venerable Bede referred to a monastery at Dacre in 698 A.D. The present St. Andrew's church stands on the site of this monastery; it lies to the right of the road as we climb the hill affter crossing Dacre Beck. Like Dalemain, with which it has close associations, the church is very well kept. A fascinating feature is that the four corners of the churchyard are marked by four carved stone bears, whose origins are somewhat obscure.

Climb out of Dacre (at 16%) and on meeting the A66 turn left. Saddleback dominates the view ahead on the return towards Keswick. Beyond Threlkeld, the mountains surrounding Keswick begin to close in, with Grisedale Pike prominent ahead. Fork left into the A591 and, ½-mile later, fork right into the A5271 to return to Keswick.

<table>
<tr><td>DAY TOUR
FROM
KESWICK – 3</td><td># The Western Lakes</td></tr>
</table>

This tour can be undertaken on any day of the week, as it is not tied to opening times, other than those of the Visitor Centre at British Nuclear Fuels, Sellafield, which is open daily from 10 a.m. to 4 p.m. (closed Saturdays and Sundays during winter) and the Lowes Court Gallery, Egremont, which is closed on Sundays and Wednesday afternoons.

THIS route covers some of the less visited lakes which are furthest distant from the popular approaches to the Lake District. It includes England's deepest lake, Wastwater, in its incomparable setting. Within a proverbial stone's thrown of each other at Calderbridge are the ancient Calder Abbey and the Sellafield/Calder Hall nuclear plant. A few miles after setting out, we traverse one of England's most dramatic mountain passes: Newlands Hause.

Leave Keswick by Main Street and High Hill. On meeting the A66, turn left and take the first turning left again (sharp left) into **Portinscale** village. The road skirts the edge of the lake by the home of Derwentwater Boat Club. As we begin to climb the hill, take the left-hand fork (signed "Buttermere") and shortly come to the entrance to **Lingholm Gardens.**

These gardens, in addition to being an attraction in themselves, give fine views of Borrowdale and are open daily.

Half a mile beyond Lingholm, take the right-hand fork — again signed "Buttermere". (The road to the left leads to Grange-in-Borrowdale and provides a short trip — suitable for an evening run from Keswick — round Derwentwater with magnificent views over the lake, especially from near Brandelhow). Near Swinside, Causey Pike appears ahead, with the Derwent Fells and the Newlands valley to the left.

At the hamlet of **Stair,** cross Newlands Beck and continue to follow the Buttermere signs. The road calls for careful driving, but the views — especially to the left — over the next few miles are magnificent. The drive over **Newlands Hause** must surely be one of the finest in England. Each side of the summit, the road has a steepness of 25%. At the summit, though only 1,095 feet high, we feel to be in the heart of the mountains with Robinson (2,417 feet) behind us and Whiteless Pike (2,159 feet) ahead, whilst the sheer crags of Wanlope to the right lead up to Crag Hill, Scar Crag and Sail. The knoll immediately to the right is Knott Rigg.

Sail Beck runs in the valley far below on the right as we descend towards **Buttermere** village. Near the foot of the descent, there is a glimpse of Buttermere lake with High Stile and High Crag rising behind. Sour Milk Gill descends from Red Pike to the foot of the lake. At Buttermere village, turn right into the B5289. The village, bound on all sides by high fells or lakes, is a centre for walkers rather than motorists.

As there are only three roads into or out of Buttermere, we must follow the same stretch of road twice. (The other occasion is on the Honister Pass run, though in the opposite direction). Much of the countryside in this vicinity is in the possession of the National Trust, including the lakes of Buttermere, Crummock Water and Loweswater. **Crummock Water** appears on the left as we leave Buttermere. The road follows its eastern shore across the foot of Grasmoor (2,791 feet), with views across the water to Mellbreak (1,668 feet).

Four miles from Buttermere, turn sharp left to Scale Hill. The road skirts the edge of **Loweswater** village before running alongside the lake of the same name. Follow the Lamplugh signs. On crossing the edge of Owsen Fell, there is a view of the Solway Firth near Maryport and of the Scottish hills beyond. At **Lamplugh Green** turn left (signed "Ennerdale"). A modern looking gateway opposite the church bears the coat of arms of John Lamplugh and the date 1595. A quarter of a mile later, fork left and continue to follow the signs to Ennerdale Lake.

Evidence of workings for iron-ore, which (with coal) forms the basis of the Cumbrian coast industry, is visible on the edge of Murton Fell. On crossing Leaps Beck, pass under the line of the former railway to the Knockmurton iron-ore mine. Situated at a height of 850 feet above sea level, this mine had an average output of 46,000 tons per year.

On breasting the edge of Kelton Fell, **Ennerdale Water** can be seen in its splendid setting, with Windy Gap (between Green Gable and Great Gable)

58

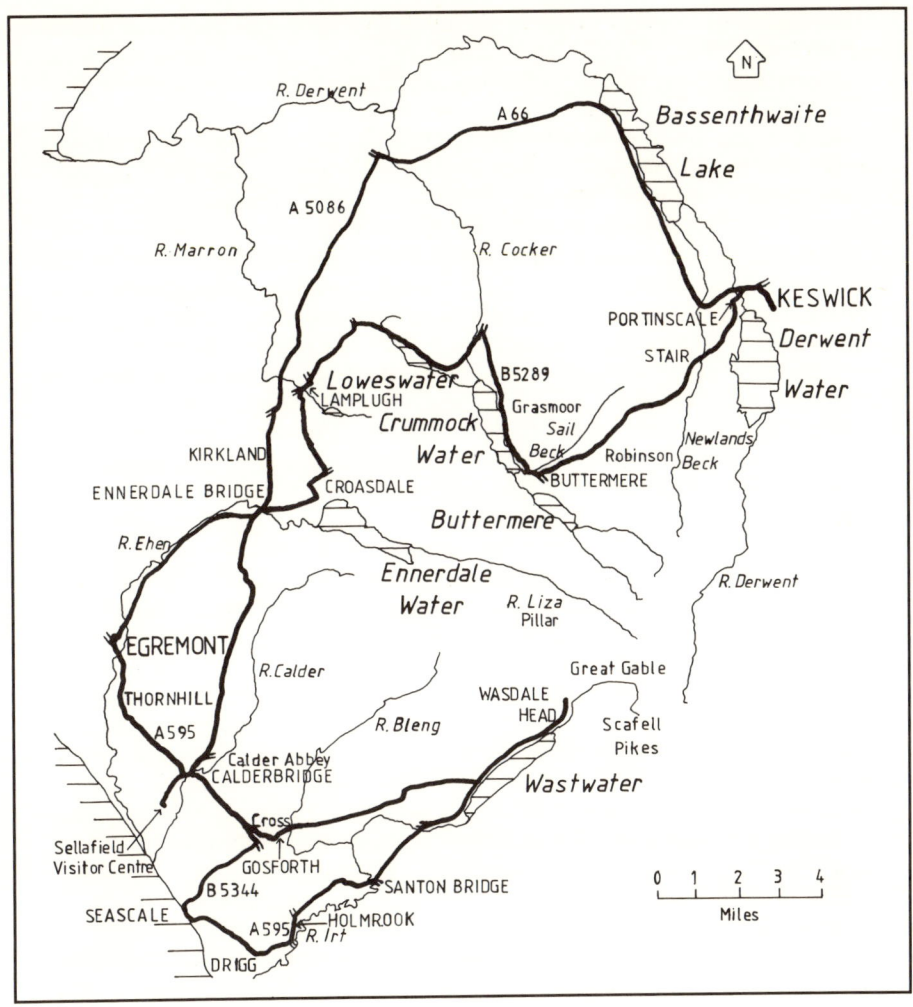

on the horizon. Ennerdale can only be explored on foot, but (like Buttermere, Crummock Water and Loweswater) it is possible to walk right round the lake. The upper valley, especially in the vicinity of Pillar Rock, is popular with climbers. At Croasdale (or Crossdale), turn right, the road to the left being a cul-de-sac for vehicles. One mile beyond Croasdale, a rough road leads to the lakeside, but again it is a cul-de-sac.

Follow the road to Ennerdale Bridge, where bear left by the school and almost ½-mile later turn left (signed "Calder Bridge"). One mile beyond this junction, **Kinniside Stone Circle** stands on the common on the left-hand side of the road. Experts vary in their assessment of its age, but one theory is that it was simply laid out by a relatively modern archaeologist to

59

demonstrate the form of prehistoric circles. From the moorland road, there are glimpses of the coast to the right, with Ennerdale Forest below; a car park and rather overgrown picnic area at **Sillathwaite** provides a convenient viewpoint.

On the descent of Cold Fell, the cooling towers of Calder Hall nuclear power station and the two concrete towers of the Windscale plutonium plant appear ahead. We now drop into the valley of the Cumbrian River Calder. At the foot of the hill, a road to the left leads to Thornholme; from this road can be seen the remains of **Calder Abbey.** The original abbey was founded in 1134/5 by Savignac monks from Furness Abbey. Little remains of the 12th century church; almost all the present ruins are of the 13th century abbey.

Turn left* by Calderbridge church into the A595 (signed "Barrow"). Half a mile beyond the Boonwood Hotel, fork left into **Gosforth** village, then left again by the Lion and Lamb Inn, and, ¼-mile later, turn left (signed "Wasdale"). St. Mary's Church stands to the left of the road. Although Gosforth has had a church for many centuries, the present building was largely rebuilt at the end of the 19th century. It does, however, contain a fine collection of Anglo-Norse stone fragments, including two Norse hogsback tombstones. Gosforth's finest feature is undoubtedly the 10th century cross, which stands 14½ feet high in the churchyard. This delicate piece of red sandstone, round at its base, but square in its upper part, is claimed to be the tallest cross in Britain and contains Norse and Christian carvings, variously interpreted, on its four faces.

From Gosforth, climb steeply out of the valley of the River Bleng and over into Wasdale, keeping left at each successive junction. We are conscious that the mountains are becoming close and eventually Scafell appears on the opposite side of the dale. The famous screes, which rise almost 2,000 feet from Wastwater, soon come into view, then the lake itself appears in the bottom of the valley. We turn left for Wasdale Head, but must eventually return to this point.

Wastwater is England's deepest lake (258 feet deep) and lies below her highest mountain (Scafell Pike, 3,210 feet high). The lakeside drive is superb, but needs to be taken with care. At **Wasdale Head,** the road divides and the triangular piece of land between the two roads serves as a car park. A short walk along the right-hand fork, which eventually leads via Sty Head Pass to Langdale or Borrowdale, leads to the tiny white-painted church, almost hidden among the yew trees. It has been suggested that the roof is partly formed from the hull of a boat, Viking-style. The church contains some carved oak panelling from York Minster.

A path runs through the churchyard to the left-hand fork near the Wastwater Hotel. Behind the hotel, a path runs alongside the Mosedale Beck, which is spanned by an ancient packhorse bridge. A footpath through Mosedale leads to Black Sail Pass and Ennerdale. Wasdale Head is one of the principal rock-climbing centres in England, with Great Gable and the

---

* If time is pressing, the route can be shortened right into the A595, then left into the Sellafield road to Calder Hall and Windscale.

60

Autumn morning on Wastwater with the mountains reflected in the still lake. The peaks, from left to right, are Great Gable, Lingmell Fell and the flanks of Scafell Pike. *(Tom Parker)*

Scafell Range near at hand.

Returning down the dale, keep to the lakeside road. Wasdale Hall, on the left of the road near the foot of the lake, is now a youth hostel. Wasdale is best seen from the foot of the lake, a spot accessible only on foot. At the first junction beyond the lake, fork left (signed "Santon Bridge"), then left again to cross the River Irt. The pretty, wooded scenery contrasts markedly with the bare screes of Wastwater.

A steep descent leads to Santon Bridge, where turn right to cross back over the River Irt by the Bridge Inn. Three-quarters of a mile later, fork left (signed "Holmrook 2"). On entering Holmrook, pass on the right Greengarth Hall, which is now a hostel providing accommodation for Calder Hall and Windscale Employees. Turn left into the A595, then, further down the village street, fork right into the B5344 (signed "Drigg"). The nature reserve contains a large colony of black-headed gulls, whilst **Drigg** village contains a mixture of local red sandstone buildings and more modern constructions.

Cross the railway by a narrow bridge to enter **Seascale,** a fresh, modern looking resort. Seascale has good sands and the breakers are said to be ideal for surfing. Pass back under the railway by a narrow arch and continue to follow the B5344 into Gosforth Road by the late 19th century St. Cuthbert's Church and the even more modern St. Joseph's Catholic Church. As the direct road from Seascale to Calderbridge is signed "Unsuitable for through traffic", return to Gosforth, where turn left into the A595 and repeat a short section of the outer journey to return to Calderbridge.

In order to visit the splendid exhibition centre of **British Nuclear Fuels** (admission free), turn left (signed "Sellafield 2") immediately past the entrance to Pelham House School, Calderbridge. After one mile, a left-hand turn leads to the Visitors' Centre. Here, the mysteries of nuclear power are simply and beautifully explained. Windscale works have been reprocessing nuclear fuel since 1952, whilst Calder Hall was the world's first commercial nuclear power station when it was opened by the Queen in 1956.

Return to the A595, where turn left and drive through Thornhill to **Egremont.** The ruined castle (admission free) stands in well-kept grounds to the left of the road. It dates from 1130 and replaced an even earlier one which stood on the large mound to the north (town) side of the present castle. Egremont is an industrial town, but has an attractive main street. The Lowes Court Gallery, housed in a 16th century building, regularly mounts exhibitions by Cumbrian artists.

Shortly after passing the clock tower, turn right into East Road and, 1/4-mile later, turn right again to descend to a hump-backed bridge over the River Ehen. Now follow the Ehen valley back to Ennerdale Bridge. Here bear right into the road from Cleator Moor. The lakeland fells dominate the view ahead on the return to Ennerdale.

For almost 1/2-mile, repeat the outward journey but in the reverse direction. (This is unavoidable unless one chooses to follow the A5086 through the rather drab towns of Cleator, Frizington and Rowrah). This time take the Kirkland road (fork left) at Ennerdale Bridge school. Beyond Kirkland, bear right into the A5086, which is followed through Lamplugh Cross. We are now in the Marron valley. **Eaglesfield,** which stands to the left of the road, was the birthplace of John Dalton in 1766, whilst a few years earlier, Fletcher Christian, the leader of the mutiny on the *Bounty,* was born at Moorland Close, almost adjacent to the A5086.

On meeting the A66, turn right. This major artery now provides a fast road back to Keswick, running along the shore of Bassenthwaite Lake, where the railway formerly had pride of place. Bassenthwaite is the most northerly of the lakes. It is 4 miles long, 3/4-mile wide, has an average depth of only 15 feet and is noted for its wildfowl. To the right lie Lord's Seat (1,811 feet) and Barf (1,536 feet), with the rocks known as the Bishop and the Clerk high above. Skiddaw (3,054 feet), with its foothill Dodd, stands on the opposite side of the valley across the lake.

The road by-passes the villages of Thornthwaite and Braithwaite. Beyond the Portinscale turn-off, turn right into the B5289 to return to Keswick.

Ullswater and Grasmere

Dove Cottage and the Grasmere Museum, Rydal Mount and the Lake District Heritage Centre, Ambleside are open daily in season.

THIS tour encircles the Helvellyn range of mountains and includes some of the most popular parts of the Lake District. It has associations with many of Lakeland's poets and writers, including Samuel Taylor Coleridge and his son, Hartley, Harriet Martineau, de Quincey, Ruskin, Southey and, of course, Wordsworth.

Leave Keswick by the A5271 — either south-eastwards via Penrith Road, then left into the A591, or north-eastwards via Crosthwaite Road. In either case, on meeting the A66, turn right (signed "Penrith"). Five miles beyond Threlkeld, turn right into the A5091 (signed "Dockray") and enter the hamlet of **Troutbeck.** Sheep markets are held in the field on the left of the road by the junction. Cross over the disused Cockermouth, Keswick and Penrith railway by the former Troutbeck station.

The hemispherical Great Mell Fell stands to the left of the road as we travel southwards. On reaching the highest point of the road (1,124 feet), the mountains of the High Street range come into view ahead, then on the descent (at 14%) to Matterdale End, the Kirkstone Pass can be seen ahead to the right. **Matterdale church** stands to the left of the road ¾-mile beyond Matterdale End. The church was built in the 16th century and restored in 1848 when the tiny tower was rebuilt. The church has a well-kept appearance; on my last visit, the churchyard, which is about 1,000 feet above sea level, was full of miniature daffodils.

The road winds through the hamlet of **Dockray,** with the Aira Beck running alongside on the left. The descent from here to Ullswater gives some of the best road views in Cumbria. Half a mile beyond Dockray, a car park, suitable for exploring Gowbarrow Park (National Trust), stands to the left of the road, whilst a second car park stands also to the left of the road almost ½-mile further. From this second car park, a short path leads through the woods to the spectacular 70-foot high **Aira Force** waterfall, where it links up with a series of footpaths through the Gowbarrow Park.

Beyond the Aira Froce car park, there are further superb views, with **Ullswater** coming into view in both directions, Place Fell rising from the water on the opposite bank and mountains all round. On meeting the A592, turn right (signed "Patterdale 3"). It was near here that Wordsworth saw his golden daffodils.

> *Beside the lake, beneath the trees,*
> *Fluttering and dancing in the breeze.*

We now run along the lake shore, with views first towards the head of Ullswater, then in the other direction as the road takes a left-hand corner between two of the lake's three reaches. Climb through Glencoyne Wood with futher views southwards along the lake. **Glenridding** is a popular lakeside village from where boats sail to Howtown and Pooley Bridge. Grisedale runs off to the right between Glenridding and Patterdale, whilst Deepdale runs parallel to it beyond Patterdale village. Both dales provide starting points for climbing Helvellyn.

Beyond the turning to Hartsop, we pass between Hartsop Dod to the left and Brotherswater to the right. The road begins to climb on the approach to the Brotherswater Inn at Kirkstonefoot, behind which Dovedale runs to the right. Caiston Beck falls steeply down between Middle Dod (the pointed one) to its left and High Hartsop Dod, which at 1,702 feet is lower than Hartsop Dod (2,018 feet).

The road reaches 1,489 feet at the summit of the **Kirkstone Pass.** Fork right into an unclassified road (signed "Ambleside") at the Kirkstone Pass

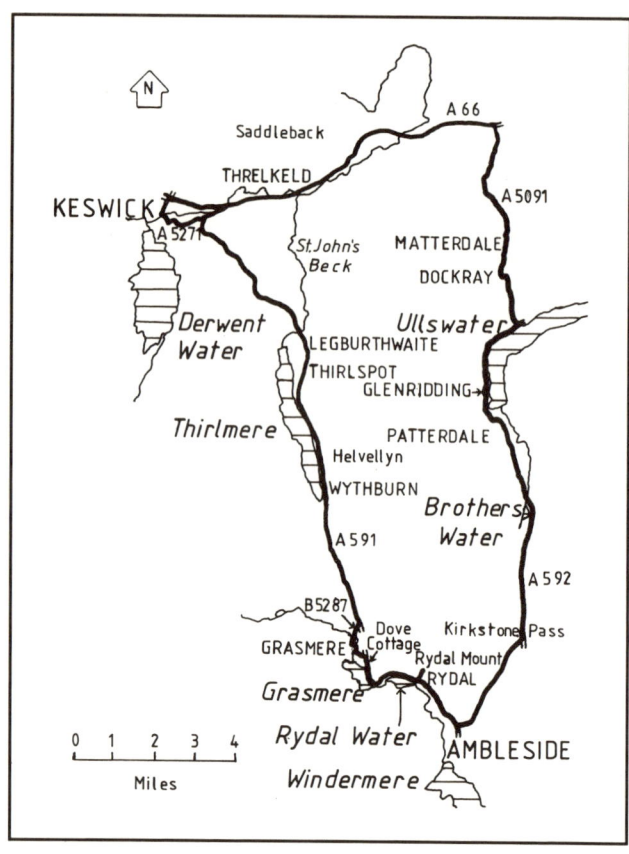

Inn and descend at 20%, with the quarries high above to the right. There is a spectacular view of Windermere ahead on descending the valley of Stock Ghyll. The road steepens to 25% on the approach to Ambleside. A left-hand turn (North Road) near the foot of the hill leads to the town centre. Alternatively, one may proceed to the foot of the hill and turn right into the A591. There is a car park immediately to the left, opposite the Charlotte Mason College.

Ambleside is a deservedly popular and beautifully situated Lake District centre. Though less than 1,600 feet high, Wansfell Pike dominates the town to the east; the mountains to the north and west are higher but not quite so close. Old Ambleside was centred on the Kirkstone road; the newer town developed progressively lower. The town is an excellent walking centre, with much holiday accommodation and a variety of shops.

St. Mary's church was built in the mid-19th century to replace the older church, which as since been converted into a parish hall. The "new" church, designed by Gilbert Scott, contains a Wordsworth chapel with windows in memory of members of the Wordsworth family. Other windows in the church are also memorials, including one installed by public subscription in memory of Matthew Arnold, who had a holiday home here, and W. E. Forster, the educational reformer. The church is the setting for the annual rush-bearing ceremony in July.

The Lake District Heritage Centre in Lake Road tells the story of man's effect on the environment over a period of 5,000 years through displays, exhibits, photographs and video films. An unusual but delightful museum is the Dolls' House Museum (open certain days) in Kirkstone Road. The National Trust Information Centre is housed in the curious, tiny Bridge House, which spans the Stock Beck. It was built in the late 16th century as a summer-house for Ambleside Hall, of which little now remains.

On leaving the car park, turn left into the A591. Between Ambleside and Rydal, the road passes through the picturesque parkland of Rydal Hall. The hall, formerly owned by the Le Fleming family, is now a Carlisle Diocesan centre and is not open to the public. Queen Wilhelmina of the Netherlands was exiled here during the Second World War.

At **Rydal,** a right-hand turn leads past the church to Rydal Mount, where Wordsworth lived from 1813 to his death in 1850. It is possible to take cars up the steep road to the house. Rydal Mount is owned by Wordsworth's great-great-granddaughter and was opened to the public in 1970 — 200 years after the poet's birth — with the assistance of a Trust. It contains portraits, items of furniture and personal possessions. The 4½ acres of gardens were designed by Wordsworth and contain numerous rare trees and shrubs. The terraces command splendid views of the fells surrounding Windermere.

A path through Rydal churchyard leads to Dora's Field, so called because it was given by Wordsworth to his daughter, who predeceased him. Continue to follow the A591 northwards past Rydal Water. Nab Cottage (to the right of the road), formerly the home of De Quincey and Hartley Coleridge, is now a quest house. At **White Moss Common,** there are car parks in the old roadside quarries, from which many footpaths radiate. Guided walks start from here on summer Saturdays.

Grasmere comes into sight on rounding a right-hand bend. The lake lies a little to the south of the village of the same name. The small cluster of buildings known as Town End stands on the A591, but one must turn left into the B5287 to visit Grasmere. Dove Cottage and the Grasmere and Wordsworth Museum stand to the right of the A591 at Town End. There is a small car park for visitors to Dove Cottage on the lane leading to the cottage and a larger public one on the right of the B5287, convenient both for Dove Cottage and Grasmere village.

Wordsworth lived at **Dove Cottage** from 1799 to 1808, a period considered by many to have produced his finest poetry. The literary associations of the cottage are enhanced by the fact that De Quincey moved in after the Wordsworths' family had out-grown the cottage and moved to Allan Bank. Dove Cottage, which was formerly a public house called The Dove and Olive Bough, must have been small in relation to the number it housed; some rooms have since been added.

A visit to Dove Cottage gives a fascinating glimpse of life there in the Wordsworth's time. De Quincey described the panelled "principal room". The walls of one of the upstairs rooms are papered with newspapers of the period similar to those hung by Dorothy Wordsworth. The garden, which is approached through a door leading off the landing half-way up the stairs, is kept in the style in which the Wordsworths laid it out.

The adjacent **Grasmere and Wordsworth Museum** was opened in 1981. It sets out William's life story with many personal relics, manuscripts and letters. The museum has already established an international reputation; in 1984-85, one of the most successful exhibitions ever to be held at the Victoria and Albert Museum, London, was mounted in conjunction with the Grasmere and Wordsworth Museum. The former museum is now a library (not open to the public).

Grasmere village lies in an incomparable setting in a heavily glaciated landscape. It is best seen from the surrounding hills, but a number of walks are possible without needing to climb very high. A particularly popular and not very strenuous walk runs round the south side of the lake and along Loughrigg Terrace to White Moss Common, giving good views over Grasmere lake and village, Dunmail Raise and Rydal Water. A favourite walk of mine commences from the Swan Hotel (on the A591), mentioned in Wordsworth's "The Waggoner". It climbs up the steep lower slopes of Heron Pike to Allcock Tarn, then descends to Dove Cottage.

The Wordsworth influence is much in evidence in Grasmere. The Wordsworths lived at Allan Bank till 1811, then occupied the Rectory for two years before moving to Rydal Mount. The simple family graves in the churchyard are seen by many thousands of visitors each year. Nearby is the grave of Hartley Coleridge, whilst Sir John Richardson, the adventurous Arctic explorer born in 1787, is also buried in the churchyard.

St. Oswald's church is worth a visit in its own right. The north arcade was

A swan provides a touch of class to the waters of Grasmere. Beyond the far shore the slopes of Loughrigg offer many pleasant walks. *(E. Emrys Jones)*

added, giving the church a "double" appearance; openings made in the original wall add to the curious effect, whilst the unusual timber roof is fascinating. Several of the yew trees in the churchyard were planted by Wordsworth. A pair of candlesticks, made by a local joiner in 1895 from one yew which fell down, are on display in the dining room at Rydal Mount.

Church Stile, a 16th century cottage opposite the church, now houses a National Trust Centre. The village is noted for gingerbread and, like Ambleside, has an annual rush-bearing ceremony. In Grasmere's case, this ancient custom is revived on the Saturday nearest to 5 August. Grasmere Sports are held annually, on the Thursday nearest to 20 August, in a natural arena at the foot of Butter Crag. They include hound-trailing, wrestling, and a guides' fell race in which the contestants can be seen from the field going up, along and down the fell.

Follow the B5287 as it winds through Grasmere village. On reaching the A591, turn left by the Swan (signed "Keswick"). Helm Crag, popularly known as "The Lion and The Lamb", stands to the left. The road now climbs over **Dunmail Raise,** named after a 10th century king or chieftain, said to have been involved in a battle here and commemorated by a heap of stones (between the two carriageways). The boundary between the former counties of Cumberland and Westmorland and even more ancient kingdoms used to pass through this point.

The tiny **Wythburn church,** described by Wordsworth as "a modest house of prayer as lowly as the lowliest dwelling", stands in trees to the right of the road near the foot of the descent. An adjacent car park provides a convenient starting point for climbers of Helvellyn, Fairfield and Dollywaggon Pike. The A591 runs along the eastern bank of **Thirlmere,** which was formed by damming the valley in 1879 and raising the water level of two former small lakes by 50 feet. The creation of this reservoir for Manchester (reached by a 96-mile long aqueduct) submerged much of Wythburn village, including the Cherry Tree Inn. Forest trails have been laid out along both shores of Thirlmere.

Thirlmere can best be seen from a small National Park car park on the left of the road, about halfway along the lake, at the point where lake and road diverge. The road now runs behind Great How (1,092 feet) which hides the northern end of Thirlmere from view. The high fells of the Helvellyn range continue to dominate the view to the right, whilst Saddleback is visible through St. John's Vale, as we drive through Thirlspot.

At Legburthwaite, the A591 turns in a north-westerly direction to cut over a low ridge before descending into the Greta valley. On the descent from the summit of the ridge near Castlerigg, there is a fine view of Bassenthwaite Lake and Derwentwater with Skiddaw (3,053 feet) on the right and Catbells (1,481 feet) on the left across Derwentwater. On entering Keswick, fork left into the A5271, which leads into the town centre.

<table>
<tr><td>LINK
ROUTE</td><td># Keswick to Carlisle</td></tr>
</table>

Mirehouse is open to the public on Wednesday and Sunday afternoons, but a lakeside and woodland walk through the grounds (for which there is a charge) is open daily.

THE route from Keswick to Carlisle is not covered on any of our day trips. The A591 leaves Keswick to follow the eastern side of Bassenthwaite Lake before it joins the A595 to cross gentle, undulating farming country to the Solway Plain and Carlisle.

Leave Keswick by Main Street (A5271 northwards), then turn right (still

A5271) into Crosthwaite Road. At the roundabout cross the A66 into the A591. There is a good view across to the Lorton Fells and Grisedale Pike and back down Borrowdale, with Castle Crag prominent. Skiddaw rises to over 3,000 feet on the right.

Bassenthwaite Lake appears below on the left. There is a car park and picnic area at **Dodd Wood,** on the right of the road, from which a number of signposted paths radiate, including one to the summit of Dodd Fell, from where it is possible to look along the lake and see Criffel in southern Scotland. Dodd Wood is a home of the pine marten. The same car park serves Mirehouse, which stands on the opposite side of the road and has associations with Tennyson. Refreshments are served in the old saw mill at the car park.

We pass St. John's church on the right, then run between **Bassenthwaite** village and the northern end of the lake. Beyond the Castle Inn Hotel, the Lake District mountains are left behind. The hills, such as the one named Binsey (to the right) at the back of the village of Bewaldeth, are now more rounded. Take a final glimpse back to the mountains as we leave the Lake Dsitrict National Park.

On meeting the A595, turn right, by-passing the village of Bothel. There are extensive views ahead towards the Solway Firth. Beyond Mealsgate, the A595 is a fast road through agricultural countryside with the town of Wigton to the left. Cross the Maryport to Carlisle railway and the River Wampool at West Woodside. The imposing gateway, with its Ionic columns, standing to the left of the road, was formerly the gateway to the now demolished Crofton Hall.

Thursby is an attractive village set around a triangular green. St. Andrew's church is Victorian, but the remains of an ancient temple have been found in the area. The village was the home of Sir Thomas Bouch, the engineer of the ill-fated first Tay railway bridge. Bear right (still A595) and soon approach the outskirts of Carlisle. Enter the city by Wigton Road and Bridge Street, crossing the bridge over the River Caldew and the railway into Castle Way.

5. North Cumbria

Carlisle lies at the point where several trunk routes meet: A74 from Glasgow; A7 from Edinburgh; A69 from Newcastle; A6 from London and A595 from Whitehaven. The M6 motorway runs within two miles of the city; leave at Junction 42 when approaching from the south.

Carlisle is also an important railway junction. Its station stands on the main London–Glasgow railway line.

FOR the purposes of this book, North Cumbria comprises all that part of the county north of Cockermouth, plus the whole of the Eden Valley.

Compared with the rest of the county, most of North Cumbria is relatively low lying, but the Pennines in the east of the area rise to almost 3,000 feet. The A689 reaches the highest point of any 'A' road in England (2,056 feet) at the Cumbria/Durham border above Nenthead, whilst Alston is one of the highest towns in the country.

In addition to the delightful Eden and Irthing valleys, the area includes the remote Kershope Forest and the southern bank of the great Solway estuary, favourite of bird-watchers and fishermen. Apart from the city of Carlisle, there are few large towns and there is little industry in the whole of the area.

Carlisle

CARLISLE is the obvious centre for touring Northern Cumbria. The city has a long history resulting from its strategic border position. It featured in numerous conflicts — Roman, Pict, Viking, Norman and medieval — right up to 1745 and changed hands between England and Scotland many times in the process. It was the Luguvallum of the Romans and became a civil settlement when they built the wall fort of Petriana at Stanwix, across the Eden.

Carlisle stands at the confluence of the rivers Eden, Caldew and Petteril. Today, the extensive riverside parkland adds to the city's attractions. Bitts Park, near the castle, houses the Cumberland agricultural show and has the usual amenities — children's playground, putting, tennis and gardens. There is a municipal golf course at Stoneyholme and a pitch and putt course on the Swifts (near Eden Bridge) whilst the county cricket ground stands on the opposite side of the River Eden. The city council has produced a leaflet about the riverside area, including a four-mile long waymarked walk.

The city centre should be explored on foot and the city council has also produced an excellent Town Centre Trail. Buildings of particular interest

The Old Town Hall, one of many buildings worthy of exploration in the centre of Carlisle.

include the splendid castle which dates from 1092, the 15th century Guildhall, the 17th century Tullie House Museum and Art Gallery, the 18th century Old Town Hall, the 19th century Court Square and Citadel (originally built in the 16th century) and the 20th century Civic Centre. The castle has always been occupied and is still in use. It contains a military museum with exhibits from the Royal Border Regiment. The Guildhall has recently been renovated and is now a museum specialising in the history of medieval trade guilds. Tullie House contains fine collections of archaeology (especially from Hadrian's Wall), natural history (especially birds) and social history.

Carlisle Cathedral dates back to 1130, the tower being added in 1401. Its nave is now very truncated, six of the eight bays having been destroyed by Cromwell's Scottish forces in 1644–45 and the stone used to repair the town walls. The building has also suffered the ravages of fire on more than one occasion. Its complete history has baffled architectural experts. The magnificent east window, though mainly 19th century, contains some original 14th century glass. The capitals on the choir pillars are carved to represent the months of the year, whilst the medieval choir stalls are one of the cathedral's finest features. The nave now houses a memorial chapel to the Border Regiment.

The cathedral was built around a monastery, said to have been established by Elfred, sister of King Egfrith. The Fratry was rebuilt in the 15th century, whilst Prior Slee's Gateway into the cathedral precinct was built in 1527. The Deanery, also early 16th century, incorporates a pele tower. Not far from the cathedral is St. Cuthbert's church with an unusual moveable pulpit and the adjacent medieval Tithe Barn, restored in 1971.

In medieval times, Carlisle had an English Gate and a Scottish Gate; English Street and Scotch Street still lead from the market place. The market cross dates from 1682; every year, in late August, Carlisle Great Fair is declared open from here. The market place becomes an open air theatre with a wide variety of almost continuous entertainment, surrounded by numerous traders' stalls, which are almost as brightly decorated as the stallholders' costumes!

In the 19th century, Carlisle became an important railway centre, with no fewer than seven railway companies sharing the Citadel station. Modern industries include fabrics, biscuits and tourism. The Sands Centre, a large new leisure complex accommodating sports, arts and social activities, opened in March 1985. The city contains a fine covered market, whilst a modern shopping centre (including an attractive pedestrian precinct called "The Lanes") has recently been created in the city centre, which has benefitted substantially from the M6 having siphoned off the through traffic. Once more the city centre is able to breathe; this, together with an apparent revival of interest in, and an awareness of, Carlisle's heritage, can only be for the benefit of residents and tourists alike.

| DAY TOUR FROM CARLISLE – 1 | **Caldbeck and the Coast** |

This tour can be undertaken on any day of the week.

THE outward journey is through the Caldew valley to the village of Caldbeck. John Peel country and the "back o' Skiddaw" are explored before skirting the northern edge of the Lake District. The approach to the Solway coast is by way of country lanes and old villages with several ancient parish churches. After visiting the coastal resorts of Allonby and Silloth, we turn inland to Holm Cultram Abbey, then follow the line of Hadrian's Wall from Bowness-on-Solway back to Carlisle.

Leave Carlisle by the Dalston Road (B5299): following the "West" signs along Castle Way, take the second turning left after crossing the railway and river. The road passes the former Dixon's cotton mill (built 1836) in

Shaddongate, which runs up Murrell Hill into Dalston Road. The Lake District fells appear ahead on the approach to Dalston.

Descend into the valley of the River Caldew past Dalston Hall. The village of **Dalston,** which was displaying a "best kept village" sign on my last visit, is a dormitory village for Carlisle with a 12th century church. Follow the road through Bridge End and Hawksdale, but where the B5299 turns right, keep straight on (signed "Rose Castle 1"). At the entrance to Rose Castle, turn left (signed "Raughton Head 1").

Rose Castle, the home of the Bishop of Carlisle, consists of a range of buildings grouped together in the 19th century around a 13th century pele tower. It is visible on the right through the trees. Cross the bridge to Raughton Head. Beyond the church, with its massive tower, bear right (signed "Lambfield") and ¾-mile later, turn left (signed "Hesket Newmarket 5"). Continue to follow the signs to Hesket Newmarket, turning left into the B5305 by the Royal Oak Inn, then right.

We are now in hilly country. Beyond Newlands, the village of Hesket Newmarket appears on the opposite side of the Caldew valley. Descend (16%) to cross the Caldew by an interesting old narrow bridge and climb up (also 16%) to **Hesket Newmarket.** This attractive village, with houses scattered around a green, was once an important market town. Bear right into the main street and pass the 18th century market cross. At the top of the street, turn right by the unusually constructed Hesket Hall (signed "Caldbeck").

Caldbeck is another charming village with old farmhouses and cottages and a busy past. Caldew Beck once drove several water-wheels for no fewer than thirteen mills, including one 42-foot diameter wheel for a 19th century bobbin mill. The village is probably best known as the home of John Peel, who is buried in St. Kentigern's churchyard to the right of the road. The huntsman owes his fame to the song written by John Woodcock Graves and the tune set by William Metcalfe. Of his thirteen children, eleven attended his funeral at Caldbeck in 1854. The church dates from the 12th century, but was beautifully restored in 1933.

From Caldbeck keep straight on up the hill, following the "Uldale" signs. At Whelpo, one mile beyond Caldbeck, a former Quaker Meeting House stands to the left of the road. Beyond Parkend we cross open moorland. Where the B5299 forks right, keep straight on (signed "Keswick 12"). The district between Hesket Newmarket and here is known as "Back o' Skiddaw"; Skiddaw appears on the left before we reach Uldale.

We catch a glimpse of Over Water in the valley to the left, then drop down (14%) to **Uldale,** yet another quiet village off the beaten track and a favourite among artists. The valley of the infant River Ellen is now crossed. Bassenthwaite Lake appears ahead 1½ miles beyond Uldale. Descend yet again, then at the Castle Inn Hotel cross over the A591 (right then left) into the B5291.

There are fine views up the Derwent valley to the left, with the central Lakeland mountains in the distance. Beyond Armathwaite Hall Hotel, with

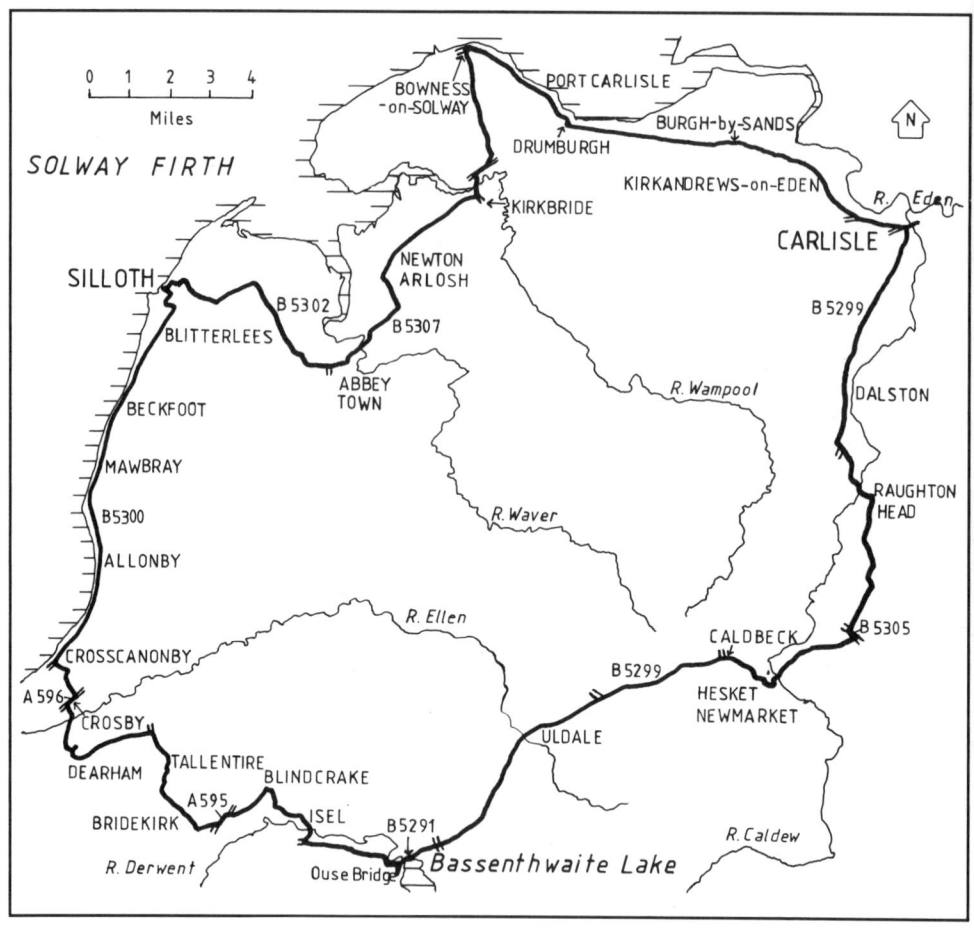

its footbridge over the road linking the hotel grounds, we run close to the northern shore of **Bassenthwaite Lake.** After crossing Ouse Bridge, it is worthwhile making a brief digression by turning left (still B5291) and parking in one of the small National Park car parks, to the left of the road, from which steps lead down to the lake side. From the shore, one can enjoy a tranquil scene to the right up the lake, with the Skiddaw range of mountains rising from the point where the River Derwent runs out of the lake.

Return to Ouse Bridge junction, where keep straight on (but note the "Give Way" sign), leaving the B5291 — our road is signed "Embleton 2½". Next take the first turning right (signed "Isel") and after one mile pass through the hamlet of Setmurthy. Some 1½ miles later, turn right (signed "Blindcrake 1¾") and descend to the River Derwent.

After crossing the bridge, keep left. Almost immediately, a narrow lane to the left leads to **Isel** (or Isell, to use the older spelling) church. The present church dates from about 1130 and has a very fine Norman chancel arch. It contains some carved stones from the 10th century or even earlier, including the Triskele Stone (on the chancel window ledge), so called because of its three-armed triskele symbol. The Elizabethan Isel Hall, built round its older pele tower, stands to the left of the road ¼-mile past the church.

On entering the village of Blindcrake, take the first turning left, then, at the next junction, turn left again. Beyond the hamlet of Redmain, turn left into the A595, then take the first turning right (signed "Bridekirk 1"). **St. Bride's Church,** which stands to the left of the road, contains a famous 12th century font, but the building was locked on my last visit. The 19th century church incorporates Norman fragments from the earlier church, the ruins of which can still be seen in the graveyard.

A mile beyond Bridekirk, turn right into the village of **Tallentire,** where you follow a one-way system. On descending the hill from Tallentire, the Scottish mountains can be seen across the Solway Firth. Be careful not to miss a left-hand turn one mile from Tallentire (signed "Dearham 2").

Dearham lies on the West Cumberland coalfield and is quite a sizeable community. It is not the most attractive village in Cumbria, but it does possess a gem of a Norman church. Turn right into Main Street (signed "Dearham Bridge 1") and shortly turn right again for St. Mungo's Church. The church contains a considerable collection of Anglo-Saxon sculptured stones, discovered by the then vicar during the 1882 restoration. Of particular interest is the "Adam Stone", which can be seen on the window sill to the left of the entrance. Near the organ stands a thousand year old cross, which tells the story of both the Norse and Christian religions; it formerly stood in the churchyard.

Returning to Main Street, turn right and follow the signs to Crosby. A steep (20%) descent with a hairpin bend leads to Dearham Bridge, where cross over the River Ellen and the Barrow–Carlisle railway. On meeting the A596, turn right into Crosby, and ¼-mile later turn left to **Crosscanonby.** The small red sandstone church of St. John the Evangelist contains a chancel arch which is thought to date from Roman times, whilst part of a 10th century,cross shaft stands in the porch. The road winds through the village, then descends to the coast, where turn right into the B5300.

The coastal road skirts the edge of Allonby Bay and gives views across the Solway Firth to the Scottish mountains in Dumfries and Galloway. The bay was formerly the home of the Cumbrian sea-salt industry and there are remains of 18th century washing and settling tanks. **Allonby** is a spacious village with a stream running parallel to the beach. It is a centre for horse riding and horses can often be encountered roaming over the green and promenade. First impressions of the village are that it is not especially appealing, but Allonby has the odd surprising corner when explored on foot. The beach is a mixture of mud and sand but is good for bathing.

North of Allonby, pass along the edge of the village of Mawbray and through the village of Beckfoot. At low tide, the sea goes out for more than a mile hereabouts. Beyond Blitterlees, pass the Stanwix Park Holiday Centre, then enter Silloth. After crossing over the former railway bridge — the railway opened In 1857 and closed in 1964 — turn left into Eden Street, then keep straight ahead along Lawn Terrace to the promenade.

Silloth is a Victorian town built on a "grid-iron" plan. It became a port in the 19th century and its front is still dominated by the flour mills. It has a wide expanse of sands and a substantial stepped promenade backed by wooded grassy knolls. A tiny miniature railway runs along the edge of the green and the promenade close to the car park. The usual holiday resort attractions include a swimming pool, paddling pool, putting, golf, tennis, bowls, facilities for riding and fishing, an amusement arcade and a children's playground.

One of Silloth's finest attributes is the splendid view across the Solway Firth to the Scottish hills, dominated by Criffel (1,868 feet). The view is particularly attractive at sunset. The Firth is a favourite haunt for fishermen and bird-watchers, the salt-marshes being inhabited by oyster-catchers, black-backed gulls and barnacle geese. Some fishermen still practise the ancient Norse custom of salmon-fishing with "haaf-nets".

Return along Lawn Terrace to the cross-roads (by the Golf Hotel), where turn left into Criffel Street. Then turn right into Petteril Street (signed "Carlisle") and follow the B5302 to Abbey Town, where keep straight ahead for **Holm Cultram Abbey.** The present building, which forms the parish church, is but a relatively small remnant of the once impressive Cistercian abbey.

The abbey was founded in 1150 from Melrose, Borders Region (which, in turn, had been established as a daughter of Rievaulx, North Yorkshire some fifteen years earlier). It has a long and fascinating history. In its complete state, the abbey was 279 feet long, 135 feet wide (in the transepts) and had a tower 114 feet high. At the time of the dissolution, it was retained as the parish church, as a result of a petition to Chancellor Thomas Cromwell on the grounds that it served as a defence against the Scots. The tower collapsed in 1600 and the building fell into considerable decay. It was restored and reduced to its present size in the first half of the 18th century, when the nave was shortened to six bays and the present walls were inserted in the arcade openings.

Today the red sandstone buildings appear to be well maintained. An information centre and shop are housed in all that remains of the cloister block and these are connected to the porch by an ambulatory. The abbey serves as a flourishing Arts Centre in addition to its main role as a church. Numerous fragments of stone from the former buildings are housed in the 16th century porch, which also protects the magnificent 12th century west doorway. Many of the houses and farm buildings in the vicinity have incorporated into them beautifully carved stones from the original abbey, which served as a ready-made quarry when it fell into decay.

Leave Abbey Town by the B5307, keeping left by the abbey (signed "Kirkbride"). After passing through Moss Side and Newton Arlosh, with its

Silloth, a spacious Victorian town, offers splendid views from its promenade across the Solway Firth to distant Criffel.

fortified church tower, we reach Kirkbride (not to be confused with Bridekirk visited earlier). At the entrance to the village, turn left (signed "Bowness 3¾"). After crossing a narrow bridge over the River Wampool, turn right and, in less than ¼-mile, fork left (again signed "Bowness") to cross Bowness Common, with the Glasson Moss Nature Reserve, noted for its rare mosses and large areas of sphagnum bog, on the right.

Enter **Bowness-on-Solway** by St. Michael's Church, then turn right (signed "Carlisle"). Bowness stands at the narrowest part of the Solway and was the site of the Roman camp at the western extremity of Hadrian's Wall. It was connected to Annan, on the opposite shore, by a railway viaduct well over a mile long, built in 1869 and demolished in 1933 after being closed in 1921 for repairs which never took place.

The road runs along the edge of the estuary — a popular spot for bird-watchers — and is liable to flooding (in which case take the B5307 from Kirkbride back to Carlisle). The harbour of Port Carlisle was built in 1819 and a canal linking the port to Carlisle itself was opened four years later, but both fell into disuse when the port silted up in the mid-19th century. The canal was subsequently converted into a railway.

A straight road runs across the marsh alongside the former canal/railway from Drumburgh, with its 16th century castle, to **Burgh-by-Sands.** Burgh was also a fort on the Roman wall. The present church was built in the centre of the fort using stones from the wall. King Edward I laid in state in the church after dying at Burgh Marsh on his way to Scotland; a memorial to him stands on the marsh. After passing through Monkhill and Kirkandrews-on-Eden, return to Carlisle, bearing left into the B5307 and passing through the suburb of Newtown.

<table>
<tr><td>DAY TOUR
FROM
CARLISLE – 2</td><td># North-East Cumbria</td></tr>
</table>

Naworth Castle is open on Wednesdays and Sundays.

REMOTE lanes are followed and a corner of the Border National Forest Park skirted, before seeing the remarkable 7th century Bewcastle Cross and exploring a section of Hadrian's Wall which includes several different features. The warm red sandstone of the Irthing and Eden valleys provided the building materials for Lanercost Priory and the market town of Brampton, both of which we see before returning to Carlisle. The whole area has associations with Sir Walter Scott.

Leave Carlisle by the A7 (signed "The North"). After crossing over the River Eden, pass through Stanwix, which was the site of the largest fort on the Roman wall, housing a regiment of 1,000 cavalry. Kingstown Road is not a very attractive way out of the city, but continue to follow the A7 (signed "Galashiels") into open countryside. Pass through the villages of Harker, Blackford and Westlinton, where cross the River Lyne.

In the middle of a wooded section of the A7, turn left (signed "Arthuret Church ¾") and at the next junction, turn right. **St. Michael & All Angels' Church, Arthuret,** which is the parish church for Longtown, stands to the left of the road. This impressive red sandstone church dates from 1609. It has an embattled roof and a solid looking tower. An ancient cross with a fragmented Maltese Cross head stands in the churchyard.

Enter Longtown by Arthuret Road, then turn left into the A7. **Longtown** has a wide main street in which stands the Graham Arms Hotel, named after the leading family in the area for centuries. Take the second turning right into Netherly Street and follow the "Netherly" signs. The road runs through the Netherly Hall estate; the hall is described by Sir Walter Scott in *Marmion*.

As I drove along this pleasant country lane one sunny autumn afternoon, at least a dozen pheasants were congregated together at the side of the road adding a splash of brilliance to an already beautifully coloured scene. At Moat Common, fork right (signed "Penton") and on meeting the B6318, turn right (signed "Catlowdy 1½").

Liddesdale lies to the left as we drive through Catlowdy and into the **Border National Forest Park.** The Park covers an area of 59,000 hectares (228 square miles) on both sides of the England–Scotland border. It includes the Kielder, Redesdale, Wauchope, Newcastleton and Kershope Forests; our road passes through a corner of the last-named. There are extensive long-distance views across the Lyne valley with the Northern Pennines beyond.

Descend to cross the Black Lyne river by a narrow bridge. One mile later, turn right (still B6318), then take the first turning left (signed "Bewcastle Church 2½") into the White Lyne valley. Cross open pasture land to **Bewcastle,** with posts to mark the course of the road in the snow. Bewcastle church stands to the left of the road. The plateau on which the church stands is the site of a Roman fort which covered six acres. This was an outpost of Hadrian's Wall, linked by a road to the fort of Camboglanna (Birdoswald), which we shall see later.

Bewcastle's main claim to fame is its fine 7th century stone cross. Apart from having lost its head, the cross is exceptionally well preserved. Each of its four faces contains finely executed carvings; a booklet, available in the church, describes these in detail. St. Cuthbert's Church dates from the 13th century and has a Georgian tower. The original building was erected from stones taken from the Roman fort, as was the castle, which occupied the north-east corner and the remains of which can be seen from the churchyard.

On leaving Bewcastle church, the ramparts of the Roman fort are clearly visible. The road now dips to cross the stream by the Lime Kiln Inn. There are good views ahead and to the right as we again cross open moorland. There are a number of fortified pele-towers in this area, reminders of the bitter years of conflict between the English and the Scots. **Askerton Castle,** which stands to the right of the road four miles from Bewcastle, is a fine example of a fortified farmhouse dating from the 14th century with later additions.

Cross over the B6318, our road being signed "Lanercost 3". Descend at 12% into the valley of the King Water, but (unusually) we are already climbing again before crossing the stream by a narrow bridge. At the next T-junction, turn left (signed "Birdoswald 3½") and climb up through **Banks** village. A converted farmhouse on the line of the Roman wall formerly housed the LYC (Li-Yuan-Chia) Museum; it stands to the right of the road at the top of the hill.

Beyond Banks, the road follows the remains of **Hadrian's Wall** for some considerable distance. The Wall was commenced in 122 A.D. and was built of whatever materials were locally available: stone in the east and turf in the west. It was 73 miles long and was linked to a series of further fortifications along the west coast. It took advantage of several natural lines of defence; the Vallum, a flat-bottomed ditch with ramparts on each side, took a more

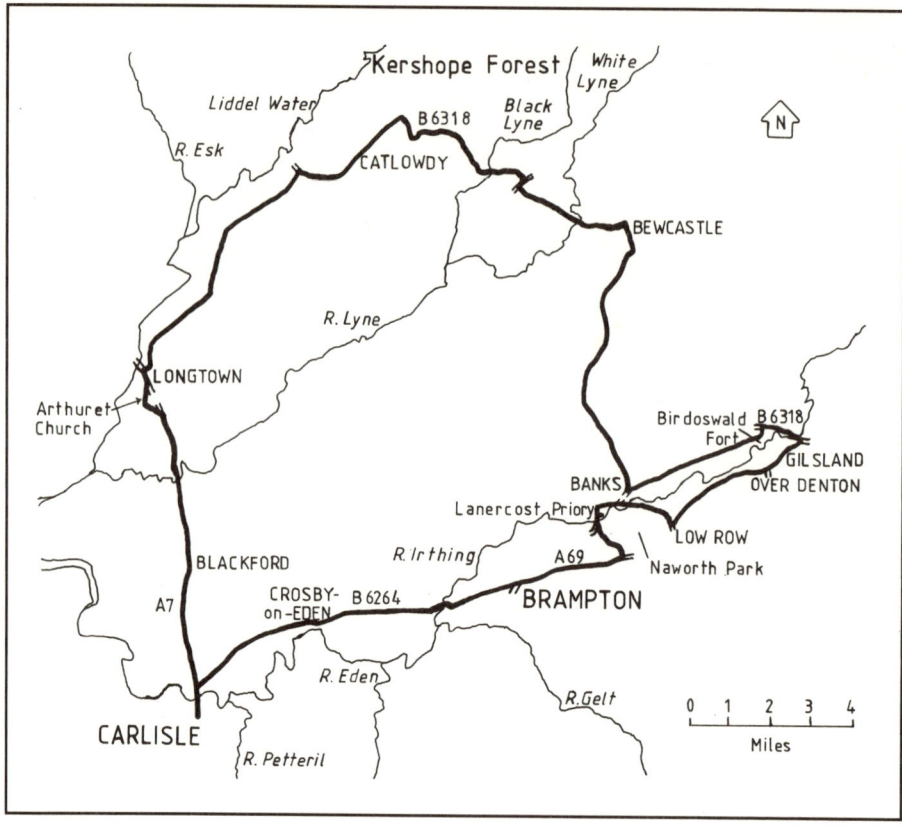

direct line south of the Wall. The Roman Wall marked the north-west boundary of the Roman Empire; it was finally abandoned in 383 A.D.

On leaving Banks, there is a fine view over the Irthing valley to the right; it is not difficult to see why the Wall was built in this position. A variety of different kinds of earthworks and remains are to be seen between Banks East Turret (on the right) and Poltross Burn Milecastle. Between each pair of milecastles (placed 1,620 yards — a Roman mile — apart) were two turrets, manned by troops from the nearest milecastle. The turrets were square look-out towers recessed into the Wall; we can see the remains of Leahill, Piper Syke and Birdoswald turrets.

A well-preserved section of the Wall leads to **Birdoswald Fort.** The site of Camboglanna camp stands just to the right of the road and is well worth a visit. The 5-acre fort is situated high above the Irthing Gorge; the view from the escarpment is spectacular. The camp was built to house 500 cavalry or 1,000 infrantrymen and was rebuilt no fewer than four times. The remains include a corn-drying kiln and some impressive outer defences and gateways. Much of the site remains to be excavated.

A further well-preserved section of the Wall runs between Birdoswald and Harrow's Scar Milecastle. Beyond Birdoswald, the road swings round to the left, but the Wall can be seen running straight ahead. On meeting the B6318, turn right (signed "Gilsland 1¼") and have further good views of the Irthing Gorge. One mile later, turn right again and cross the Irthing into **Gilsland,** where keep right following the "Brampton" signs. Gilsland featured much both in Scott's writings and in his life. It was here that he met and proposed to Charlotte Carpenter. In the 19th century, sulphur and chalybeate springs were discovered and the village became a spa.

At the top of the hill out of Gilsland, Hadrian's Wall reappears on both sides of the road. A good walk alongside the Wall, to the right, leads to the **Willowford Roman bridge** abutment, passing Willowford East and West turrets on the way. The abutment stands across the Irthing from Harrow's Scar Milecastle. To the left of the road, another footpath leads across the field and over the railway to **Poltross Burn Milecastle.** The remains, on the steep west bank of the burn, clearly show the layout of the milecastle. The burn itself forms the boundary between Cumbria and Northumberland.

Resuming our tour, cross the Newcastle–Carlisle railway at Denton School crossing. Keep close to the track, keeping straight on (signed "Brampton 8"), where the main road turns left one mile from Gilsland. The first village we come to is **Over** (or Upper) **Denton**; its tiny Norman church stands across the railway and appears to be no longer in regular use for worship. The chancel arch is made of Roman stones thought to have been taken from Birdoswald.

Our road now crosses back over the railway. Nether Denton's Victorian church also stands to the right of the road. At the T-junction by Low Row signal box, turn right (signed "Lanercost 2¼") and descend again into the Irthing valley. Beyond Birkhurst, the road both steepens and narrows. After crossing the bridge over the River Irthing, turn left to Lanercost, where a further left turn leads to the priory.

Cars may drive through the interesting arch of the former gatehouse to **Lanercost Priory.** The red sandstone priory was established as an Augustinian foundation in 1166 and was attacked several times by the Scots between 1296 and 1346. The nave of the priory is exceptionally well preserved and is still in use as the parish church with regular candlelight services being held. The monastic quarters are less well preserved, but there is a fine restored west range, including a pele tower, known as Dacre Hall, as Sir Thomas Dacre made this his home when the buildings were given to him by Henry VIII at the time of the Dissolution.

On leaving the priory, turn left and cross the Irthing by the "new" bridge. The fine, two-arched medieval bridge, with its protective cutwater base, stands to the right. Turn left into a narrow road immediately after crossing the bridge. This road runs through Naworth Park and passes the entrance to **Naworth Castle.** The 14th century castle, with a central courtyard, was built by the Dacres, but passed through the female line to the Howard family. Its most famous occupant was Lord William Howard, known as "Belted Will".

The castle was faithfully restored after a fire in 1844. It is still owned by the Earl of Carlisle and is now open to the public. .

On meeting the A69, turn right (signed "Carlisle"). Enter the attractive red sandstone town of **Brampton** across a triangular green. On the right-hand side of the green at the far end is an enormous motte (known locally as "The Mote"), over 100 feet high, on top of which a statue to the seventh Earl of Carlisle was erected in 1870. At the foot of the hill, turn left into the town centre.

Brampton is well worth an exploration on foot and a well-designed leaflet describing a town trail has been produced by the local amenity society. The market square lies off the main road and contains an interesting octagonal moot hall. The present building dates from 1817 and was altered in 1896. Outside the Moot Hall are some iron stocks.

Brampton's original Norman church stood on the site of a Roman fort about a mile west of the present town centre. The present St. Martin's church was built in 1874 by the Earl of Carlisle. Its unusual design (by Philip Webb) must have been revolutionary at the time it was built. The church is particularly noted for its brilliant stained-glass windows, designed by Sir Edward Burne-Jones and made by William Morris.

A market charter was granted to Brampton by Henry III in 1252. Bonnie Prince Charlie stayed in the town when he received the surrender of Carlisle in 1745. Not long afterwards, cotton-weaving was established in Brampton; there are still some former weavers' cottages in the town. A by-pass for the heavy A69 traffic is currently under consideration.

Leave Brampton by the B6264 (signed "Carlisle Airport") at the foot of the town. This is a quieter road than the A69; it runs across Crosby Moor and through Crosby-on-Eden. Enter Carlisle at Stanwix. On meeting the A7, bear left over the Eden Bridge to return to the city centre.

DAY TOUR FROM CARLISLE – 3	# The Eden Valley

This tour can be undertaken on any day of the week, but in view of its exceptional length, as long a day as possible should be allowed. Both Acorn Bank garden and Appleby Castle are open daily in summer.

THIS full-length tour of the Eden Valley can be made practicable by using the fast M6 motorway for the return journey. The Eden Valley is exceptionally beautiful throughout its length and to omit any section would be to do it less than justice. Because of its proximity to the popular Lake

District on the one hand and the Pennines and Yorkshire Dales National Park on the other, it is quieter and less well-known than one might otherwise expect. It is a particularly fertile valley with rich, deep red soil.

Leave Carlisle by the A69 eastbound: by Warwick Road or Victoria Place, which runs into Warwick Road. Brunton Park, home of both Carlisle Soccer and Rugby League teams, stands to the left of this road. Cross over the M6 motorway, and, at the cross-road in Warwick village, turn left into a lane signed "The Old Chapel". A short footpath leads from this lane to **St. Leonard's Chapel.** This church, reconstructed in Victorian times, contains an original Norman arch and a fine French-style Norman apse.

On returning to the A69, turn left and descend the hill to the River Eden. Turn right into the B6263 immediately before the bridge. After a short riverside drive, climb up to the attractive village of **Wetheral,** where, at the triangular green, fork left. Where the road to the left descends to the church, bear right into a narrow lane which runs past the ruined gatehouse of the former **Wetheral Priory.** The Priory was founded in 1100, but none of the original buildings remain. The gatehouse dates from the 15th century.

Corby Castle can be seen standing on the opposite side of the River Eden from near the Priory gatehouse. The large stone lions in the castle roof represent the arms of the Howard family. The River Eden runs through a picturesque gorge between Wetheral and Corby. Immediately beyond the Priory gatehouse — just before the road turns to the right — a kissing gate leads to a series of paths through **Wetheral Woods** (which are owned by the National Trust) and down to the river. One path (keep straight on, then bear left — not sharp left) leads to some stone steps which descend to caves carved out of the steep bank. The caves, which are approached across a short wooden bridge and through an iron gate, are said to have been occupied by St. Constantine and are known as St. Constantine's Cell.

A statue of Constantine stands on the opposite bank of the river immediately opposite. Close by is a medieval salmon weir and salmon traps which are still in use. The Eden is a paradise for fishermen throughout most of its length and contains salmon, trout and grayling.

At the next T-junction turn left, then take the next turning left (signed "Armathwaite 6"). There are views of the long line of Pennine fells to the left. For several miles, the road runs through the "Royal Forest of Inglewood", which formerly stretched from Penrith to Carlisle and covered an area of almost equal width. The Eden Valley is particularly attractive between Wetheral and Langwathby, but in parts its full beauty can be better appreciated by rail than by road. The line through the Eden Valley must rank as one of the most scenic stretches of railway in the country. We cross back over the railway at Low House crossing.

The low, red sandstone Chapel of Christ and St. Mary stands to the right on entering **Armathwaite** village. The church dates from the 12th century but was rebuilt in the 17th century after being used as a cattle shed. Keep straight ahead through Armathwaite, but it is worth making a short digression to the River Eden (follow the "Ainstable" sign). From the bridge the riverside castle can be seen to the right. This is a pele tower with substantial Georgian and Victorian additions.

Pass through a Gothic archway under the railway, then turn left (signed "Plumpton") and, 300 yards later, left again (signed "Lazonby"). The Eden lies in the trees below to the left. Continue to follow the "Lazonby" signs: after 3½ miles, turn left and, ½-mile further (by Lazonby Hall), turn left again. Cross over the railway and enter Lazonby by the village sheep market. **Lazonby** is an attractive red-sandstone village with an open-air heated swimming pool and adjacent riverside picnic area. On meeting the B6413, turn right, then, after passing under the railway bridge, turn left into the B6412 (signed "Great Salkeld").

One mile beyond Lazonby, a drinking trough, which stands to the right of the road, serves the unusual dual purpose of commemorating the Coronation of King Edward VII in 1902 and the lessening of the gradient of Scatterbeck Hill. The River Eden and the Settle–Carlisle railway can be seen to the left as we run through this fertile agricultural part of the valley.

St. Cuthbert's church stands to the left of the road in **Great Salkeld** village. The porch, which contains fragments of Saxon stonework, protects the fine Norman doorway, with its zig-zag arches and strange carvings. The Norman chancel archway is equally fine. The church contains one of the best examples of a fortified tower. This massive, embattled tower is built like a castle keep. The thickness of its walls can be seen by examining the windows of the tunnel-vaulted ground floor room, approached by means of a doorway (with an exceptionally strong 14th century door) from the nave. A dungeon lies beneath this strongroom, whilst a spiral staircase (locked on the occasion of my last visit) leads to a first-floor room which, I understand, contains a fireplace. The tower was clearly built to serve as a refuge in the border wars. A colourful window in the nave contains a portrait of St. Cuthbert with two scenes from his life. Near the altar is an old stone effigy of Thomas de Caldebec, dating from the early 14th century, whilst on the wall above the door leading to the tower are some examples of 17th century armour.

Two miles beyond Great Salkeld, keep straight ahead (signed "Langwathby") where the main road turns to the right. On meeting the A686, turn left and cross the River Eden to Langwathby. The large, narrow girder bridge appears to be a temporary structure, but has been here for some time. **Langwathby** (pronounced "Langanby") is quite a pretty village spread around a green. Keep right at the green (still A686) and, 300 yards further, turn right into the B6412 (signed "Culgaith 3½").

We cross over the railway again and have agreeable views to the right over the River Eden near its junction with the River Eamont. On entering Culgaith, turn left, then at the next junction, turn right (in both cases, signed "Appleby"). The road descends at 12½% to a level crossing by the former Culgaith station.

Three-quarters of a mile later, immediately after crossing over Crowdundle Beck, turn left (signed "Acorn Bank") into a streamside lane. **Acorn Bank** house is now a Sue Ryder Home, but the walled garden

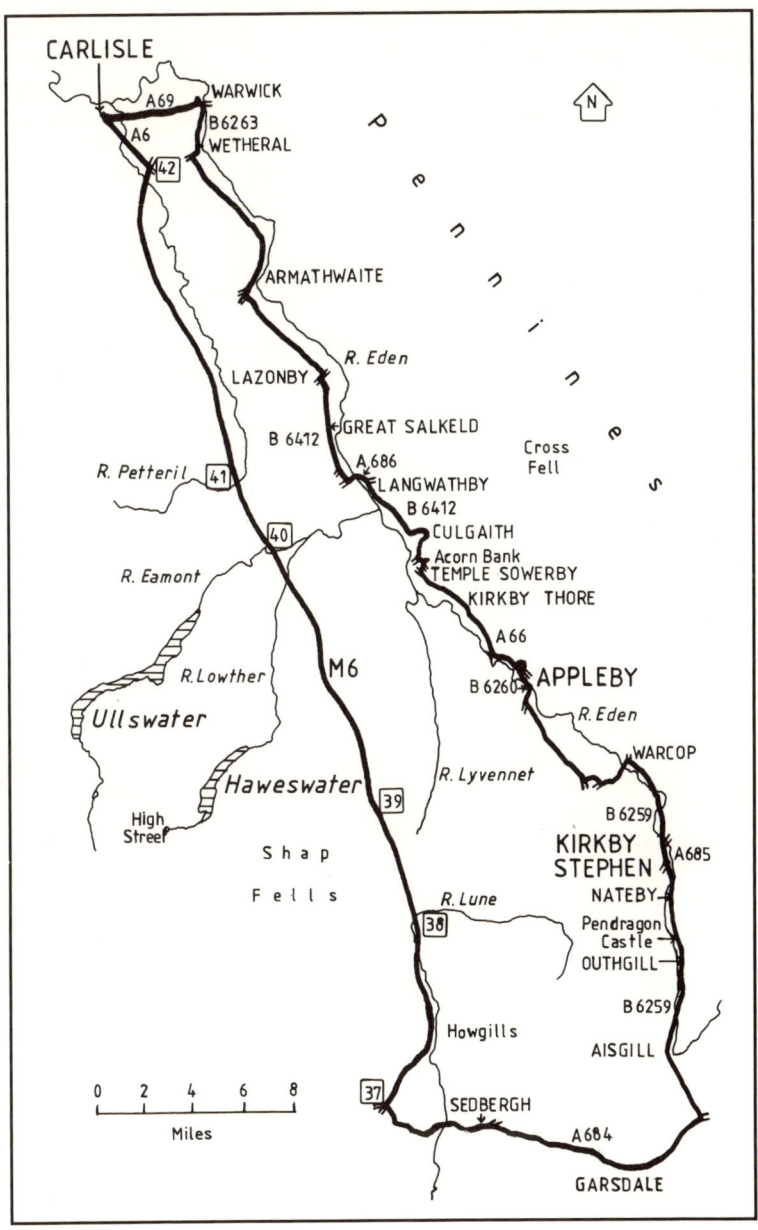

CARLISLE

WARWICK
A69
B6263
A6
WETHERAL
42

ARMATHWAITE

R. Eden

LAZONBY

GREAT SALKELD
B 6412
A 686
LANGWATHBY
B 6412
CULGAITH
Acorn Bank
TEMPLE SOWERBY
KIRKBY THORE
A66
APPLEBY
B 6260
R. Eden
WARCOP

Cross
Fell

R. Petteril
41

40

R. Eamont

M6

R. Lowther

Ullswater

Haweswater

R. Lyvennet

39

High
Street

B 6259
KIRKBY
STEPHEN
A685
NATEBY
Pendragon
Castle
OUTHGILL
B 6259
AISGILL

S h a p

F e l l s

38

R. Lune

Howgills

0   2   4   6   8
37
SEDBERGH

Miles

A684

GARSDALE

P e n n i n e s

N

(National Trust) is open to the public. It is noted for its medicinal and culinary herbs and its spring bulbs. There are picturesque views of the beck from the back of the house.

On leaving the grounds, turn left, then take the first turning right into the village of Temple Sowerby. Keep left on entering the village green, then straight on past the parish church of St. James. **Temple Sowerby** is a small but captivating red sandstone village with an air of spaciousness. On meeting the A66, turn left.

Half a mile south of Temple Sowerby, in a lay-by on the left-hand side of the A66, stands a Roman milestone surrounded by an iron railing cage. **Kirkby Thore,** which stands to the left of the A66, was the Roman fort of Bravoniacum. A Roman camp also stood close to the junction of the road to Long Marton. We run along the edge of Crackenthorpe village, then immediately after passing under the railway line, fork left into the B6542 and keep left following the "Appleby" signs. The road runs under the A66 into Appleby-in-Westmorland.

At the foot of the hill, turn right into the B6260 and cross the bridge over the River Eden into the town centre. Since the opening of the A66 by-pass, **Appleby** has reverted to being a quiet market town. Before the former county of Westmorland was absorbed into Cumbria in 1974, Appleby was its county town. It was granted its charter in 1179 and in the 13th and 14th centuries it was a much larger and more important town than it is today.

Boroughgate, the main street of the old town, is a delight. It has quite a steep slope and is flanked by treelined greens behind which stand buildings with a variety of colours of facings. Near the bottom of the street stands the 16th century Moot Hall, on an island in the street itself, slightly off-centre, as at Keswick, Bridgnorth and elsewhere; at the top of the street stands the castle. At each end of the street stands a tall column or cross, the High Cross being older than the Low Cross.

St. Lawrence's church stands at the foot of Boroughgate. The earliest part, the foot of the tower, is Norman, but the rest of the Norman church was destroyed by the Scots. The organ, one of the oldest in the country still in use, has recently been restored. The church contains the tomb of Lady Anne Clifford, whose influence on the town can still be seen. St. Anne's Hospital in Boroughgate, now almshouses, was built by Lady Anne, whilst St. Michael's church in Bongate, now closed, was considerably restored by her.

Appleby Castle was one of several Clifford family castles, others being at Brough, Brougham, Pendragon and Skipton-in-Craven. It occupies a strategic position overlooking the Eden. Its Norman keep, with later frills, is particularly well preserved. The keep and grounds are open to the public during the summer months; the grounds contain a conservation centre of the Rare Breeds Survival Trust, which houses a variety of unusual birds and farm animals. On the second Wednesday in June and the previous day, the town is virtually taken over by what is claimed to be the largest horse fair of its kind in the world.

Amongst the literature available from the Information Centre, housed in the Moot Hall, are a town trail and a leaflet describing the ties between Appleby's historic school and the Washingtons of Westmorland county, Virginia, U.S.A. A plaque on Appleby railway station marks the spot where the late Eric Treacy, Bishop of Wakefield, died whilst enjoying his favourite pastime — photographing trains.

Leave Appleby by the B6260, which runs from the top of Boroughgate, past High Cross and the castle into Shaws Wiend, then bears right into Parkin Hill. One mile from Appleby, at the edge of the village of Burrells, turn left (signed "Ormside 2"). Keep straight ahead to Helm, where we cross the railway and Helm Beck.

Take the next turning left (signed "Warcop 2¾") into a narrow lane and enjoy further views of the Pennine fells to the left. Continue to follow the "Warcop" signs through the hamlet of Bleatarn and descend to cross the Eden by a 16th century bridge, said to be one of the oldest bridges in the country still in regular use. **Warcop** is also noted for its annual rush-bearing ceremony which takes place on St. Peter's Day (29 June). Turn right into the B6259 and in the five miles between Warcop and Kirkby Stephen, cross the Eden a further three times.

On meeting the A685, turn right into **Kirkby Stephen.** This stone Pennine market town can be a little bleak and windswept, but is not unattractive. There are some fine Georgian buildings in Kirkby Stephen and its vicinity, whilst the town contains a surprising number of present or former places of worship in addition to the magnificent parish church of St. Stephen. Known as the "cathedral of the Eden Valley", the church dates from the 13th century, with an early 16th century tower and later additions. It contains various tombs and monuments to members of the Musgrave and Wharton families, whilst a modern engraved-glass window depicts the stoning of Stephen. The church is approached from the market-place by means of the Cloisters, a 19th century colonnade. Kirkby Stephen received its market charter in 1350.

Leave Kirkby Stephen by turning left from Market Street into the B6259 (signed "Nateby 1½"), passing the 1856 Temperance Hall just beyond the turning. Between Kirkby Stephen and Nateby, we again cross over the Eden, this time near Stenkrith riverside park and Coup Kernan Hole, into which the whole river pours itself. On the wall of the Black Bull Inn at Nateby, a circular A.A. village sign (of a type once very familiar) is still displayed.

We now follow a quiet road through the Upper Eden valley; an unfenced section of this road runs close to the river. The remains of **Lammerside Castle** (on the opposite side of the Eden) are scanty, but the ruins of **Pendragon Castle,** which stands to the right of the road by the junction with the road from Ravenstonedale, are quite impressive. Originally a fortified pele tower, the castle was destroyed by the Scots in 1541 and rebuilt by Lady Anne Clifford in 1660.

The village of **Outhgill** is the centre for the scattered district of Mallerstang. Its church was also rebuilt by Lady Anne. Beyond Outhgill we

Kirkby Stephen, a market town at the head of the Eden Valley, boasts this attractive 19th century colonnade which provides the approach to the church from the market-place.

are conscious of the high hills all around as the valley narrows. Mallerstang Edge lies to the left and Wild Boar Fell to the right. The road follows the course of an old drovers' road from Scotland to the markets of Northern England. The infant River Eden and the Settle–Carlisle railway, both of which we have followed all the way from Carlisle, are close at hand.

The **Settle–Carlisle line** was built by the Midland Railway in the 1870s to provide a third main line to Scotland in competition with the West Coast and East Coast routes. Its construction was to first-class standards and it was a remarkable feat of engineering. Aisgill viaduct stands to the right just before we cross over the railway. Aisgill Summit (1,169 feet above sea level) is the highest point on the line, which is the highest main line in England. At the time of writing, this splendid line is threatened with closure.

The River Eden rises in the fells to the left. It flows down the deep ravine of Hell Gill and through a series of waterfalls, the lowest of which can be seen on the opposite side of the railway at **Aisgill.** This small waterfall can be quite spectacular when in spate, especially when high winds blow the spray over the bleak moorland. At Aisgill we cross from Cumbria into North Yorkshire and enter the Yorkshire Dales National Park.

There now begins a descent through bare countryside, winding either side of the railway. Shotlock Hill and Moorcock railway tunnels, with Lunds viaduct sandwiched between them, illustrate the heavy engineering of the Settle–Aisgill section of the line. At the isolated Moorcock Inn, turn right into the A684 (signed "Sedbergh 10"). We now pass under the railway and return from North Yorkshire into Cumbria. Dandry Mire viaduct, on the left, was originally planned to be an embankment, but thousands of tons of materials disappeared without trace into the mire and the plans had to be changed. Garsdale station stands to the left at Garsdale Head.

Garsdale village, with its tiny church rebuilt in 1861, lies two or three miles down the dale from the station. The road crosses the Clough River several times as it winds through the dale. Baugh Fell rises to over 2,200 feet on the right, whilst Rise Hill (1,825 feet) separates Garsdale from Dentdale on the left. Despite its small population, Garsdale has produced a number of eminent men of learning, including John Dawson, mathematician and doctor, James Inman, expert in navigation, and John Haygarth, who began isolation hospitals and introduced smallpox vaccine into the U.S.A.

At the foot of Garsdale, we cross the Dent fault. The geology changes from the limestone and Millstone Grit of the central Pennines to the older rocks of the Lake District. There is a short section of unfenced road on crossing Garsdale Rigg below Longstone Fell, some two miles before Sedbergh. The dome-shaped Howgill and Shap Fells dominate the scene to the right and ahead of us. Cross a narrow bridge over the River Rawthey to enter Sedbergh. At the T-junction, turn left and continue to follow the A684 through the town. Traffic is now routed to avoid the narrow streets of the town centre.

Sedbergh is perhaps best known for its school, founded in 1525 by Roger Lupton. We pass some of the buildings and the well-kept, spacious playing fields. The town was formerly both a woollen and cotton manufacturing centre. St. Andrew's Church is Norman with later additions, including a 15th century tower. As with many churches nowadays, it was locked on the occasion of my last visit. The vicinity of Sedbergh has been a stronghold of both Quakerism and Methodism. A National Park centre has been established in the town and a town trail leaflet is available.

Beyond Sedbergh, the Vale of Lune is entered (still A684). After passing St. Gregory's Church, the Dales Way long-distance footpath, which runs from Ilkley (West Yorkshire) to Bowness-on-Windermere, crosses the road. Immediately beyond the Dales Way crossing, negotiate the narrow Lincoln's Inn Bridge, which spans the River Lune. At this point, we leave the Yorkshire Dales National Park.

Climb steeply (16%) out of the Lune valley up the slopes of Firbank Fell. The Howgills dominate the view back to the right, whilst from the summit there are views to the left over Killington reservoir. It should be borne in mind that stopping is not allowed on motorways, so if the driver wishes to consult the text for the rest of the tour, he should do so now.

Turn right into the M6 (signed "The North"); it is 44 miles back to Carlisle from this point. This is no ordinary motorway; the road from here to Junction 40 is one of the most spectacular sections of motorway in Britain. The Lakeland fells can be seen to the left, whilst Whinfell Beacon (1,544 feet) is surmounted by a G.P.O. aerial of extra-terrestrial appearance. The Dales Way crosses the M6 by its own special footbridge.

The Crewe–Carlisle section of the West Coast main line to Scotland runs to the right, whilst beyond it can be seen the viaduct of the former "little" North Western line from Clapham (North Yorkshire) to Lowgill. We now enter the **Lune Gorge,** through which the M6, A685, railway and River Lune squeeze side by side — or, more accurately, stepped above each other. Even the two carriageways of the motorway are separated. The former "railway town" of Tebay stands to the right, whilst the above-average Tebay West service area lies to the left a little further north.

The M6 reaches its highest point (1,036 feet) at **Shap summit** just before Junction 39. There are further views of the Pennine fells to the right, whilst Saddleback can be seen in the distance to the left. At Clifton, a 16th century fortified farmhouse can be seen to the right of the motorway. Beyond Junction 40, we pass Penrith (also on our right) with its beacon surmounting the hill behind.

Whereas the outward journey followed the River Eden and the Midland railway, the return journey from Penrith to Carlisle follows the River Petteril and the West Coast railway. We again pass through the remains of Inglewood Forest. At Junction 42, beyond the Southwaite service area, leave the motorway and return to Carlisle by the A6 through Carleton and Harraby.

DAY TOUR FROM CARLISLE – 4	Alston and the North Pennines

Little Salkeld Watermill is open from 2.30 p.m. to 5.30 p.m. on Monday, Wednesday and Thursday from Easter to September, plus additional days in August. Aim to be at Little Salkeld not much later than 2.30 p.m. if Corby Castle grounds (which close at 5 p.m.) are also to be visited.

THE town of Alston lies on the eastern side of the Pennine watershed and is linked to the rest of Cumbria by a single road — the A686. In order to avoid retracing the journey, we shall stray over the border into Northumberland on the outward journey. The return is via the high Hartside Pass, with its splendid views over Cumbria and beyond, then includes visiting a restored working watermill, seeing an enormous Bronze Age stone circle and enjoying the grounds of a country home.

Leave Carlisle by the northbound A7 and keep in the right-hand lane on crossing the wide Eden Bridge. Immediately beyond the bridge, fork right into the B6264, Brampton Road. At the time of writing, this is confusingly signed "A69" when approached from the south. Pass the Cumbria College of Art and Design on the left; Rickerby Park stands between the road and the River Eden to the right.

Four miles from Carlisle, the village of **Crosby-on-Eden** is reached. The Victorian red sandstone church of St. John the Evangelist, which stands to the left of the road, has an unusual short tower. The present clear windows were installed in 1957 and are surmounted by the original attractive tracery windows with cut-glass star motifs. Immediately opposite the church, turn right (signed "Little Corby 2½").

The Pennine Fells appear ahead as we drive towards Newby East. On entering the village, turn right into a narrow road (signed "Little Corby ¾"; easy to miss) and cross over the River Irthing, just above the point where it flows into the Eden. On entering Little Corby, turn left by the Haywain Inn into another narrow opening (signed "Corby Hill"; also easy to miss).

At Corby Hill, cross over the A69 and take the first turning left (signed "Hayton"). One mile further, pass on the left **Toppin Castle,** which now appears to be a farmhouse but incorporates an imposing pele tower. Follow the "Talkin" signs, which means keeping straight ahead, 1½ miles beyond Toppin Castle, where the main road bears right. We now descend into the picturesque valley of the River Gelt. A riverside path runs through Gelt Woods and close to a former quarry which contained inscriptions made by Roman quarrymen.

After crossing over the River Gelt, pass under Gelt Bridge, a three-arched viaduct carrying the Newcastle–Carlisle railway. (Despite the inscription on the viaduct, this, though old by railway standards, is not Roman!) Cross over the B6413 into a narrow road, which leads to **Talkin** village. Talkin's simple but appealing neo-Norman church stands on the road which runs to the right from the cross-roads in the centre of the village.

Two hundred yards beyond Talkin cross-roads, fork right (signed "Hallbankgate"). As we climb up out of Talkin, there is a lovely view to the left over Talkin Tarn and the Irthing valley. **Talkin Tarn Country Park** (which can be approached from the B6413) is a popular spot for sailing, rowing, fishing, swimming, riding and walking.

At Hallbankgate village, bear right by the Belted Will Inn into the A689 (signed "Alston 15½"). This remote corner of Cumbria contains evidence of former coal-mining and quarrying activities. Beyond the village of Midgeholme, we pass into Northumberland and, a mile beyond Halton-Lea-Gate, cross the **Pennine Way.** This 270-mile long footpath runs from Edale in Derbyshire to Kirk Yetholm, just over the Scottish border. For several miles south of Halton-Lea-Gate, the Pennine Way closely follows Maiden Way, a Roman road which runs southwards from Hadrian's Wall.

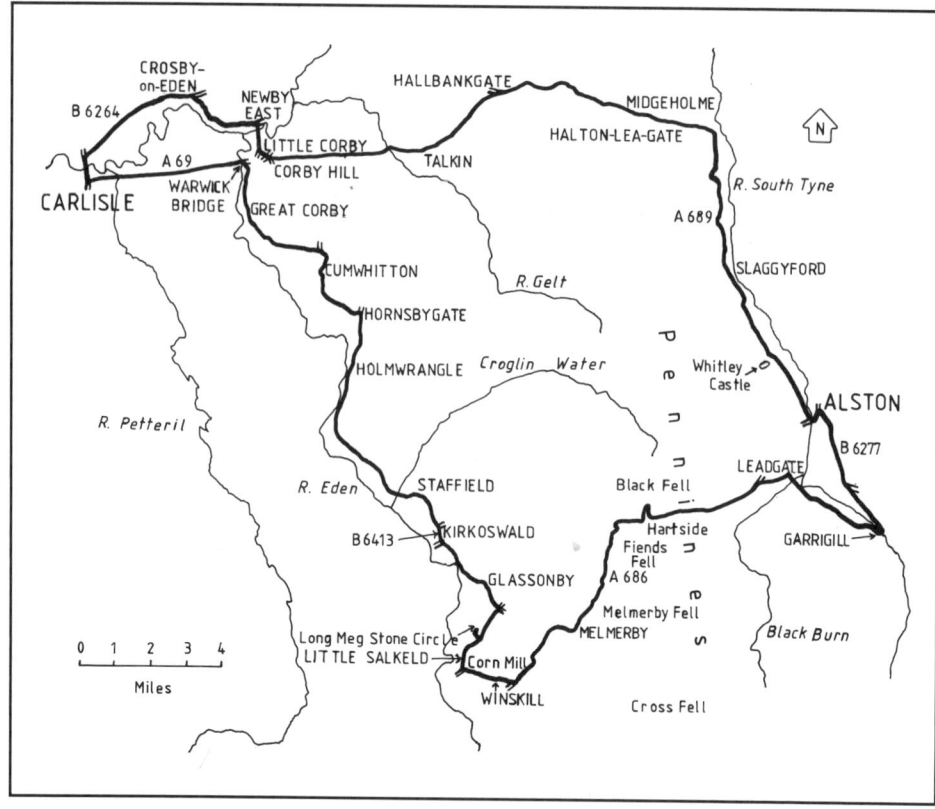

At the edge of Lambley, our road (still A689) turns southwards into the South Tyne valley. The Pennine Way is crossed several times between here and Alston. The South Tyne flows through many pretty wooded reaches to the left. Some 2½ miles south of the village of Slaggyford, the Pennine Way leads through a farmyard to the right of the road (opposite a telephone kiosk) and passes close to the ramparts of **Whitley Castle.** This Roman fort was an outpost of Hadrian's Wall.

A little further south, we cross Gilderdale Burn to return to Cumbria. Shortly afterwards, Alston appears ahead, slightly to the left. On entering the town, bear left, then on meeting the A686 turn left and cross over the South Tyne into the town centre. Alston stands at the confluence of the South Tyne and the Nent and in many ways, including the local dialect, is more akin to Northumberland than to Cumbria.

Alston should be explored on foot. Narrow streets and alleyways lead off from the cobbled steep main street (A689) which runs up past the Town Hall, church and market cross. A number of the older houses have outside staircases. St. Augustine's church is known to have existed for over 800 years, but the present building was erected in 1870. Its predecessor had lasted only 100 years. An interesting feature is the "Derwentwater Clock" near the entrance. The clock is thought to date from the 16th century and was moved to the church from Dalston Hall in 1770, having previously belonged to the Earl of Derwentwater. The former Gossipgate chapel is now an art and craft gallery, whilst the former grammar school is now a fire station.

For 2,000 years Alston was a centre of mineral mining, especially lead, though copper, silver, iron and anthracite were also mined in the area. Its importance diminished with the decline of the mines, but the town has gained in popularity in recent years as a tourist centre, particularly among fell walkers for whom it makes an ideal base. Its other attractions include fishing, golf, riding and pony-trekking. The railway line from Haltwhistle was closed by British Rail in 1976, but was re-opened as a narrow gauge line by the South Tynedale Railway in 1983. At present, trains run only as far as the county boundary at Gilderdale Bridge, but there are plans to extend the line farther down the South Tyne valley.

Both Alston and the Peak District town of Buxton claim to be the highest town in England. Whilst parts of Alston are higher than parts of Buxton, the Derbyshire town probably has the stronger claim overall. Both towns lie in hollows with higher hills all around. The village of Nenthead, with which Alston was linked by a remarkable 5-mile long canal tunnel built by John Smeaton in 1810, stands 400 feet higher just within the Cumbrian boundary.

Leave Alston by the A689, but at the top of the main street keep straight ahead into the B6277 (signed "Barnard Castle"). Evidence of past mining activities lies all around. Primitive Methodism flourished amongst the former mining communities, especially in Alston, Nenthead and Garrigill. Two miles beyond Alston, fork right and descend to the secluded South Tynedale village of Garrigill.

Bear right at the George and Dragon Inn (signed "Leadgate 3"). **Garrigill,** which lies on the Pennine Way, is an old stone village spread around a triangular green. As at Alston, the church records date back several centuries, but the present building dates from the 18th century and was much restored 100 years later. The interesting building with an outside staircase on the green is now a private residence, but was formerly the village smithy and blacksmith's shop.

Beyond Garrigill, there are views over the infant South Tyne valley. At the village of Leadgate, cross the Black Burn, then turn left (signed "Penrith 17"). One mile later, bear left into the A686. The road climbs through bleak moorland to over 1,900 feet at **Hartside Cross.** Conditions here can change very quickly in winter; the tall posts are to mark the edge of the road in snow.

From the summit, there is a magnificent view over the Eden valley to the Lakeland fells. The A686 provides a spectacular introduction to the Lake District for visitors from Northumbria; the watershed would make a more natural county boundary than the existing one. Hartside Summit lies between Fiends Fell to the south and Black Fell to the north. Cross Fell

Alston — like Buxton! — claims to be the highest town in England. Its steep main street climbs past the church and market cross.

(2,930 feet), the highest point in the Pennines, lies some five miles south of Hartside.

The road is sub-Alpine in character as it zigzags down from the Hartside cafe. It eventually winds into the village of **Melmerby,** with its spacious green and well-known village bakery. The red sandstone church of St. John the Baptist is hidden away behind Melmerby Hall and should not be confused with the tower house on the green. Melmerby sometimes finds itself in the path of the Helm Wind, a phenomenon peculiar to the Eden valley. The north-east wind, rushing over the edge of the eastern escarpment, produces in the right circumstances a situation in which violent, destructive winds upwards of 90 m.p.h. can be experienced, whilst literally in the next field the air can be quite still! The wind often lasts for several days over a 25-mile line running north-east from Brough, almost always east of the River Eden.

At a cross-roads 2½ miles beyond Melmerby, turn right (signed "Winskill ½") and, ¼-mile later, fork left into Winskill village. At the next T-junction, by the former Little Salkeld railway station, turn right. **Little Salkeld Mill** stands to the right of the road just after crossing the bridge on entering the village. Visitors can see flour being stone-ground in the traditional way. The mill, which is powered by two 12-foot waterwheels, was restored in 1975. The adjoining seven acres of land are farmed organically on a rotation basis; the mill itself uses only organically grown English wheat. The watermill contains a shop and tearoom.

At the top of Little Salkeld village street, turn right (signed "Glassonby") and, ½-mile later, turn left (signed "Long Meg"). **Long Meg and her daughters** is the name given to a stone monolith and some 59 (at one time, there were more) smaller stones arranged in an oval over 100 yards in diameter. This early Bronze Age monument is the largest in the country after Stonehenge.

Return to the cross-roads, where turn left and, at the next cross-roads, turn left again into Glassonby. Keep left through this quiet village and descend at 14% into the valley of the Hazelrigg Beck. As we approach **Kirkoswald,** the detached Victorian bell-tower can be seen standing on top of the hillside beneath which the church shelters. It is said to have been built separately because of a spring underneath the chancel which made it impossible for it to be placed on the building, but the fact that the bells can be heard in the village much better from the top of the hill than the bottom is to me a more appealing explanation. St. Oswald's church itself dates from circa 1300.

Kirkoswald is an alluring village. Little is now left of the castle (which stands in a clump of trees near the road to Park Head), much of the masonry having been used to build the village and also to build Naworth Castle for the Dacres, into whose possession Kirkoswald came. The house known as The College is so called because it replaced a college for priests which was founded here in 1523 and dissolved by Henry VIII. Opposite the entrance to the College, a path leads to the church.

On meeting the B6413, keep right (signed "Croglin"). The village street of **Kirkoswald** contains a number of inns, whilst a tiny, cobbled square containing the village war memorial lies off the street to the left. At the top of the street, keep straight on past the Methodist church, whilst the B6413 turns right. Keep left through Staffield, passing the hall on the left. As we climb up (at 16%), **Nunnery House** is passed, also on the left. The 18th century house, built round a 13th century core, is set in 35 acres of grounds through which the Croglin Water passes in a deep, dramatic gorge before joining the Eden. Attractive footpaths are open to the public for a small charge. The Nunnery rapids on the River Eden are popular with canoeists.

A pretty, wooded road along the eastern side of the Eden valley is now followed. The village of Armathwaite can be seen ahead across the river; at Armathwaite Methodist church, fork right, then left (signed "Holmwrangle 1½"). The River Eden now runs close beside us to the left. Keep left at each successive junction, taking care not to miss the left-hand turn at Hornsbygate (signed "Cumwhitton 2"). Do not, however, take the turnings to Hornsby and Moorthwaite, both of which are cul-de-sacs.

Cumwhitton is a charming village. The ancient St. Mary's church is kept locked, but appears to be well-kept, as is the churchyard. The church has an outside staircase leading to the tower. Beyond Cumwhitton, turn left again (signed "Great Corby 2¼"). The grounds of **Corby Castle,** which stands to the left of the road, are open to the public. The castle itself (not open) is 17th century, but, as so often in these parts, incorporates an earlier pele tower. The gardens were laid out in the early 18th century. Great Corby is a conservation village.

Beyond Great Corby, the road runs alongside the River Eden. At Warwick Bridge church, keep left, then, on meeting the A69, turn left opposite the entrance to Holme Eden Abbey. Cross the 1837 bridge over the Eden to Warwick. The A69 passes Carlisle Golf Club (on the left) before crossing over the M6 to return us to the city centre.

LINK ROUTE	**Carlisle to Bowness-on-Windermere**

THERE is a choice of routes from Carlisle to Bowness-on-Windermere. Leaving Carlisle by the A6 (southbound), we may either join the M6 at Junction 42 or follow the A6 through Penrith.

The shortest route leaves the M6 at Junction 40, then takes the A592 (signed "Ullswater"), which leads off the westbound A66. The section from Ullswater to Bowness is described in reverse in the opening part of Chapter 3 — Day Tour 2 (page 20). This route is not suitable for towing caravans.

An alternative route leaves the M6 at Junction 39 and joins the A6 just south of Shap. The section from here to Bowness via Burneside is described in the closing part of Chapter 3 — Day Tour 2 (page 24). The latter part of this route is not suitable for towing caravans.

A second alternative route leaves the M6 at Junction 38 and follows the A685 from Tebay to Kendal. The section from Tebay to Bowness is described in reverse in the opening part of Chapter 3 — Day Tour 5 (page 37).

Drivers towing caravans might prefer to leave the M6 at Junction 39, then take the A6 to Kendal, the A5284 and A591 to Windermere and the A5074 to Bowness.

Now turn to Chapter 3.